Mom on the Run

PREPPING FOR LIFE'S EMERGENCIES
WHEN YOU'RE AWAY FROM HOME

Mom on the Run

Karen S. Morris

Copyright © 2023 Karen Morris

All rights reserved. This book or any portion thereof may not be reproduced or used in any manner whatsoever without the express written permission of the publisher except for the use of brief quotations in a book review.

Dedication:

Valerie Jones

Mom, there is so much that I want to say to you, but let's begin with, "Thank you." Thank you for always being there for me. Thank you for your listening ear. Thank you for bolstering my spirits when things are tough and for celebrating with me when things are going well.

But saying, 'Thank you," isn't enough. You need to know that you have been an inspiration to many – to Jo, to me, to Jordan and Shannen. We see what you've walked through, and the manner in which you've walked through it. You inspire us to keep going when things look bleak. You remind us that we can overcome when things appear insurmountable. You point us to God when we're tempted to turn away. You are the epitome of a strong woman. I want you to know that we see and admire that strength in you.

You will forever be one of my heroes. I love you.

CONTENTS

Acknowledgments ix
Introduction xi

SECTION ONE: EVERYDAY CARRY 1

Chapter One–Defining EDC and Delineating its Benefits 3
Chapter Two–Creating Your Own EDC 11
Chapter Three–7 Categories of EDC 20
Chapter Four–EDC Organization, Review, Upgrade, and Training 33
Chapter Five–Helping Others with EDC and Vehicle Preparedness 48
Section One Addendum – EDC Checklist 52

SECTION TWO: THE PREPARED VEHICLE 55

Chapter One–Defining the Prepared Vehicle and Delineating its Benefits 59
Chapter Two–Being Prepared for "Around-Town" Emergencies 66
Chapter Three–Vehicle Preparedness for the Long Haul 80
Chapter Four–Seasonal Vehicle Preparedness 95
Chapter Five–Vehicle Organization 105

Addendum 117
Conclusion 123
What's Next? 127
Endnotes 133
Bibliography 135

ACKNOWLEDGMENTS

Steve, two books in one year! It's like having twins again for the third time. We survived it twice and came through stronger. This should be a walk in the park.

To my kids, I want you to know that I'm proud of your hard work. I'm so pleased with your determination. Stay focused, follow God, and love those around you.

To Kit, thank you for listening when I needed to talk. Thank you for speaking things to me in a way that I felt cared for. I appreciate you. I trust you.

To my readers, thank you all for your e-mails and messages. Thanks for your support and encouragement.

INTRODUCTION

> "Long-range planning does not deal with future decisions, but with the future of present decisions."
>
> — Peter F. Drucker

According to the 2019 American Time Use Survey, fifty percent of our waking hours were spent at home. That means of our waking hours, we also spent fifty percent of our hours away from home! That's a staggering statistic.[1]

My own life bears that out. In today's society, we are always on the go. Each week when I fill out my Prepper Planner, there's rarely a day when I don't have to leave the house. It's funny because even my eleven-year-old has stopped asking me, "Is anyone going anywhere tomorrow?" He knows that I will. His question has changed to, "Is anyone else going out with you tomorrow?" Because he gets it: I am always on the go. That's not how I want to be, but for this time in my life, that's how it is. It's everyday life.

But what about special occasions? This year alone, I've been to North Carolina for a week, Pensacola, Florida for nine days, and Omaha, Nebraska for almost two weeks. I'm also planning to go to Orlando, Florida for a week. As I added it up, by the end of 2022, I will have been gone from home for over a month!

How about you? Does a day go by when you don't leave the house? Do you go out multiple times a day? How many trips do you take during the year? One, two, four, more?

So, when we're on the go so much, the commensurate problem is that we're away from the majority of our preparedness supplies. If you're at home and you spill part of your meal down your shirt, it's not a big deal—generally. You remove the shirt and treat it. When you're at home, if you need to go to the bathroom, you go. It's not a big production. When you're at home and cut your finger, you have peroxide and Neosporin and Band-Aids. You have everything at your fingertips.

That's not necessarily the case on the go. We have to make sure that we have systems in place to care for our needs and the needs of those around us when we are away from home.

That's where *Mom on the Run* comes in. There are four layers to our preparedness when we are on the go. We have what is on our person, what is nearby our person, what is quickly available, and what is in our vehicle. Throughout this book, we're going to tackle two main topics: Everyday Carry (also known as EDC) and Vehicle Preparedness.

We're going deep into each of these topics. We'll break EDC down into seven different categories and drill down into each. What does each category look like? How does having each category of EDC benefit me? How do I easily carry everything I need without lugging a huge purse or backpack around? How do I organize my preparedness supplies so I not only know exactly what I have, but exactly where to find them?

Then we're going to work through Vehicle Preparedness. I know in my own life—if I took the hours that I'm away from home in my vehicle and the hours I'm away doing various activities, whether church, or grocery shopping, or running errands (if you don't count my hours of going to a coffee shop to work on my business)—I spend more time in my car than I do at all of my combined activities.

Considering how many hours I spend away from home, that's a significant statistic. It also means my vehicle needs to be ready to meet my needs and my family's needs at a moment's notice. In *Mom on the Run* we take that seriously. We break Vehicle Preparedness into seven areas and examine each. What do the categories look like in a vehicle as opposed to on our person? What kinds of things can and should I keep in my vehicle to be ready for each type of emergency? What does vehicle organization look like?

How do I personalize my Vehicle Preparedness, and how do I always know where to find everything I need?

Why are we going to walk through these subjects? We're going to cover each subject not just so you can gain knowledge—it's much more valuable than that. When you're prepared, you're bold and confident! When you're prepared, you remove worry from the equation. When you've taken the time to formulate, execute, and evaluate that plan's effectiveness, even if the world around you is crumbling, your spirit will be able to rest knowing that you've done everything you could do to ensure your family's safety while you're on the go. So turn the page, and let's jump into how you can be prepared for all of life's little around-the-town emergencies.

SECTION ONE

EVERYDAY CARRY

> "Success is where preparedness and opportunity meet."
>
> — Bobby Unser

As a young mom, I mastered the art of Everyday Carry. Back then, I called it a diaper bag, but the concept remained the same no matter what I called it. That bag was filled with almost everything but the kitchen sink. I started developing that EDC by asking myself the question: "What did I need to make it through a trip out of the house with twins?" I needed diapers, wipes, a changing pad, burp cloths, bottles, powdered formula, binkies, extra clothes, toys, snacks, my keys, my wallet, a water bottle for me, and the list could go on ad infinitum.

Did I use each of these items every time I went out? Nope. If it was a quick trip to the store, I might not need the changing pad and extra diapers, but I might need those toys. If we were going to my mom's house, I wouldn't need the toys or the snacks. She had me covered there, but if we were there for more than thirty minutes, I would need the changing pad, wipes, and diapers.

I didn't need everything in that bag every time I left the house, but that bag would remain stocked with the same items whether or not I thought I would need it for that trip. Why? Because that trip to the grocery store might lead to a trip to the mechanic, and then I would be up the creek without a paddle if I didn't have formula and bottles if it was time to feed the twins. Or, I might plan an afternoon at my mother's house, and she suggests going to the park with the twins. Well, then I need a bunch of the items that I hadn't planned to use. The idea was to be prepared for anything that the twins threw at me—no matter which end it came from.

EDC is the grown-up version of your diaper bag. And while kid's needs are less likely to be at the center of what I pack in my EDC arsenal, they can still factor into the equation. Just like a diaper bag, there are things that you will use almost every time you are out – your phone, your wallet, and your keys. But I often find that I need other items. Today, while I was out, I got a hangnail. I needed to clip it, hence I needed a nail clipper. It's the middle of winter, and my hands are often dry. I carry a small tube of lotion in my bag. I will often work from a location outside of my house, and I hate having to pack a separate bag with all of my work needs, so I carry earbuds, a phone charging cord, and my computer's charging cord with me. I keep a stash of tampons and pads in my purse. I hate getting caught out and unexpectedly needing those 'necessities.'

Do I use each of those items every time I leave the house? No. There are a few things that are in my purse that I rarely use, but there are times when those items have saved my – or someone else's – hide.

So as we dive into this portion of the book, think of EDC as the continuation of your diaper bag days - more sophisticated, more stylish, but hopefully, just as helpful as you go about your day.

CHAPTER ONE

DEFINING EDC AND DELINEATING ITS BENEFITS

> "Start where you are. Use what you have. Do what you can."
>
> — Arthur Ashe

In A. American's Survivalist series premier book, *Going Home*, Morgan Carter is away from home for his job. While he's on the way back to his family, every electronic device or anything that has electronic components is knocked out. He has to traverse 250 miles on foot with only what he has with him. The book chronicles the trials he goes through, the people he meets, the problems he faces, and the debauchery that takes place around him. What sets this apart from many other books in the genre is that he has to go home with only the items that he has on his person, bag, and car—which of course no longer works.

But Morgan is a prepper, and while he's low on some supplies, he has much of what he needs to survive the trip for two reasons. The first is he was on a trip and had some things with him. The second is that there were items he carried on his person all the time. These items are referred to as EDC, or Everyday Carry.

WHAT IS EDC?

EDC is having the tools that you use regularly on your person, the tools that you occasionally need at a hand's reach, and the tools or equipment that you want from time to time quickly accessible.

Tools you use regularly

If you were a nurse working in a doctor's office, each day when you started your shift you would carry specific items while you worked. You'd probably have a stethoscope draped around your neck, a penlight in your pocket, a watch with a second hand on your wrist, and perhaps a small pad of paper and a writing utensil. Each of these items would help you do your job. If you take blood pressure manually, you'll need the stethoscope. If you take a pulse manually, you'll need your wristwatch with a second hand. If you're checking pupils, you'll need the penlight.

Whether you're a nurse or a mom, you have tools that you need to carry with you daily to do your job.

Let me give you a rundown of a typical day I see as a homeschooling mom.

After I get up and shower, I usually spend some time working through my day. Maybe this particular theoretical day includes a vision therapy appointment for one of my kids, a trip to Goodwill, home for a quick lunch, chess club, followed by an appointment at the house for one of the various projects on the farm, a quick dinner, and closes with work on a writing project.

So, I head to vision therapy and wait with one child in the waiting room doing school, while another child is doing their vision therapy. While we're waiting, the child I'm helping with school realizes that he's forgotten a pencil, so I pull one out of my purse for him or her to use. While we're waiting, I use my phone to answer a couple of e-mails.

When we finish with vision therapy, we run to Goodwill. While we're at Goodwill, my daughter scrapes her arm on a stray hanger, and it starts bleeding. I pull out a disinfectant wipe to clean the area, some "Neo-to-Go" to keep the germs out, and then a Band-Aid to cover the scrape.

Then we'll head home to catch a quick lunch and work a little on school. While we're home, we have a package delivered, so I pull out my pocketknife and use it to open the package.

After a couple of hours at home, we'll head to chess club. When we get there, one of my kids might accidentally kick a chess piece underneath a cabinet. I rummage through my purse or backpack to grab a flashlight so we can see the piece and extract it.

By the time I get home that afternoon to meet with the contractor for the appointment, I pull out a small 4x6 notebook and my pencil (which I returned to my purse after loaning it to said child earlier in the day), and take notes as we walk the property going over the project we have in mind.

As I'm making dinner, I realize that we're almost out of garlic (we use garlic all the time in our cooking), so I pull out my phone and add garlic to my grocery list app. And as the kids watch a movie or play a game that evening, I pull out my laptop to work on my writing project, but realize that my phone, which I'm using to listen to a quiet playlist on Spotify so I can concentrate above the din, is almost out of battery. Since I don't want the phone in the other room where I can't listen to it as effectively, I pull out my battery charger and cord and continue listening right where I am.

All day long, I've used different pieces of equipment to do my job. Just like a nurse uses a stethoscope, wristwatch, and penlight, I use a pocketknife, flashlight, Neosporin, Band-Aid, phone, small notebook, pencil, and portable phone battery charger. Those are some of my tools.

Where is your EDC kit—AKA the Three Levels of EDC

There are three levels of EDC—three "places" in extending proximity that you keep your EDC: on your person, at hand, and nearby. (There is actually a related fourth area, but we'll cover that in the next section.)

On your person

Some tools should always be on your person. In other words, they shouldn't be in a purse or backpack, and definitely not in your car.

Why? Once, I saw a woman I knew using her pocketknife to cut an apple. I remarked that it was nice to see another woman with a pocketknife. I mentioned that I kept my knife in my purse and pointed to it across the room. The woman's husband said, "What good is that knife going to do you if you need to protect yourself if it's in your purse and your purse is across the room?" And he was right.

There are some things that should just be kept on your person—usually, that means that it's in a pocket or clipped by a D-ring to a belt-loop. For me, it's my pocketknife, my keys—which have a flashlight and pepper spray attached—and my cell phone.

At hand's reach

There are some things that I keep at hand's reach. Even as my EDC has morphed over the years, some things don't change. In my purse—which is now bigger than it used to be—I keep my wallet, gum, Band- Aids, lemon packets, lavender essential oil, clip-on sunglasses, an external battery pack, and charging cord. Whenever I leave my vehicle, my purse goes with me, whether it's into a store, a restaurant, church, or another family's home. While it's not actually always hanging across my body, it's always at my fingertips.

Quickly accessible

Quickly accessible for me means that I can get to it quickly. This may mean that it's in the same room as I am, or if I'm in a store, it's in my vehicle. My backpack, where I keep my full EDC kit, weighs between five and ten pounds, so I don't carry it everywhere with me. But the things that I use most often I keep in my purse, and barring an extreme emergency, I can always get to my full pack quickly.

BENEFITS OF EDC

"EDC" used to refer to the firearm and its various accoutrements which many men carried every day. Then it was considered what you already carried with you every day. More recently, it's morphed into what you *should* carry with you every single day. A Reddit user in the /EDC subreddit, Tim Hayes, said, "EDC has been crucial to me. To be prepared is to be in control. It's not like I expect zombies to pop out of the ground or terrorists to attack. It's all the things that we run into in our daily lives that make us feel powerless when they happen. I take back control and power by having the tools I need when I need them." And that really is your EDC in a nutshell. It's having the tools you need when you need them. It allows you to take back power and no longer feel helpless. You have what you need to take control of your day.

Take back control

We just mentioned the first benefit of EDC: when you have a filled-out EDC, you take back control, and you're prepared. It doesn't matter if you're at work or at home or at the grocery store. Wherever you are, your everyday carry is with you, and that allows you to be prepared and in control of almost any "everyday" situation.

When we first moved to Central Illinois, we were at a chess club in Morton. While we were there, a young man ran into our chess club holding two knives and screaming, "I'm going to kill everyone." Yes, this really happened. If you don't believe me, you can find an article on it here: https://www.fox32chicago.com/news/illinois-army-vet-saves-16-kids-from-knife-wielding-teen-reportedly-plotting-mass-murder. You feel powerless and helpless when something like that happens. You can have tools on you, even in a situation like that, whether it's mace or pepper spray (being in a public library, we couldn't carry a firearm) that you can use to disarm someone. These tools allow you to take more control over the situation.

Help others

Using your EDC also allows you to help others. There have been a couple times that I've been sitting in church and I felt someone tap my shoulder, and the person in the row behind me said, "Do you have some Advil?" They knew I keep it on me. When we lived in Ferguson, Missouri, we were at our favorite library in St. Peters, Missouri. Someone had fallen on the carpet and got a rug burn. I was able to pull out my lavender essential oil to help the burn. When we've been out and about with our kids, sometimes one of them would fall and scrape their knees. I'd clean the wound, put Neosporin on the cut, and apply a Band-Aid (and/or ace wrap to keep gauze in place if the area was too big for a Band-Aid) because I keep those things with me.

Save time

It also allows me to save time. If I hadn't had the Advil for the person who had tapped me on the shoulder in church, that person would have had to go find some Advil in the church first aid kit, but they would have needed to leave the service, go find the first aid kit, take the Advil, and come back to their seat, missing at least five minutes of the service.

When we lived in Missouri, we were looking at properties in the country. One day for about five hours we visited several properties one after another, and at about lunchtime, we ended up at a property in the middle of nowhere. We didn't realize just how far out it was. My mom (who has diabetes) and five hungry children needed food.

Because I'm prepared, I had snack items with me. If we had had to wait a couple of more hours, my mom would have had blood sugar issues. It also saved us time. We didn't have to stop looking at properties and head forty-five minutes back toward the highway, find a restaurant, get everybody food, and return. It was so much easier because we had things with us to tide us over until we were able to get back to the highway and a restaurant.

Save money

When you plan ahead, you save money. Let's say that someone has a bad headache while you're on a trip and you don't have basic first aid items. If you decide to stop at the next gas station to get something, you'll be surprised. While gas stations carry Advil, Tylenol, and other OTCs, they come in a pack of two, and each pack costs around $1-$1.50. If you plan ahead and keep a first aid kit with you in your EDC, you'd pay around $2 for 30 or more ibuprofen or acetaminophen. Crisis averted, and money saved!

Personal expression

EDC is also a form of personal expression. Taking your EDC and truly making it your own speaks to who you are, how you roll, and how you change over time. Of any area of preparedness, my EDC is the one that I can most easily change and most reflects who I am and what I'm about at this point in my life.

At another point in my life, my backpack went with me absolutely everywhere. When I took it into another person's house, it wasn't far from my person. The older I get, the fewer places it goes with me, so now I carry more in my purse.

For some people, carrying a firearm is a part of their EDC. Last weekend, I took a concealed carry class. We already had one handgun, and I had shot it before, but taking a class with a bunch of other people showed me so many different types of handguns—and there was one out there that was a much better fit for me. It had less kick. The handle was a little larger, which meant it was easier to grip, both of which meant I was more accurate. The ammunition is also cheaper than what it costs for the handgun that we already own. This other gun and its features speak more to who I am, what I need, and what I can best handle at this point in my life.

There are other ways your EDC can speak to who you are. One of my favorite pieces of EDC is my knife. I like it so much I have two backups. It's interesting, I've gotten a lot of comments on my knife. I don't take it out often, but when I go to the chiropractor, I take it out of my pocket so I'm not laying on it. My chiropractor has commented on how pretty it is—the blade has almost a rainbow sheen to it, and it's very pleasant to look at. It speaks to the fact that while I'm a prepper, I'm also a woman and like pretty things.

The fact that EDC gives us a chance to express ourselves also means it gives us a chance to change things as we find something that fits us better.

Recap and Looking Ahead

In this chapter, we discovered the concept of EDC. We defined Everyday Carry. We discussed the three levels of EDC and how having different levels makes us better prepared. We finished the chapter talking about EDC and its many benefits.

In the next chapter, we're going to delve deeper. We're going to discuss how you can develop your own personalized EDC. What do you need on your person? How is that different from what I might need to carry in a purse or backpack? Yes, there will be some overlap, but no two person's EDC will ever be exactly the same. Turn the page and get ready to start cultivating your own tailor-made EDC.

CHAPTER TWO

CREATING YOUR OWN EDC

> "Consistent progress. Learn and improve every day. You'll always look back and be thankful for the effort that you put into yourself."
>
> — Author Unknown

Most brides spend countless hours and obscene sums of money in preparation for their wedding day. Afterall, a wedding is one of the most important events in a woman's life. According to the website, The Ascent, in 2020 most couples spent around $30,000 on their wedding.[2] While of tantamount importance, a wedding is one day out of our lives. If, as women, we're going to spend that time, money, and energy on making sure one day is perfect, taking even a portion of that time to make sure that every excursion is at least minimally taken care of, makes good sense.

When it comes to creating your own EDC which will allow you, at a minimum, to take care of basic needs, there is no one size fits all. Everyone's days look different. I no longer have little kids at home. You may have three "littles." I live on a hobby farm. You may live in a big city. I work from home. You may stay at home with your kids or go to work. Our days and our tools will not look alike. You want to be ready for what *you* are likely going to face, not what I'm going to deal with.

So to the end of helping you develop your own EDC, I'll offer a series of questions. As you answer these questions, use them to decide which pieces of equipment you want to carry. Each step along the way, you'll be creating your own personalized EDC.

Before you begin, I want you to start a list or document called "EDC." You can do this in your grocery shopping app, in a document on your phone, or on a piece of paper. As you work through these questions, when you think of something you should keep with you, add it to your list. The idea is to use items we already have around our house first. But there may be a few items you decide you need to purchase. Once your list is made and you've gathered the items you already have, as you go shopping, pick up one or two of the items you need to buy. Build your preparedness arsenal simply and easily.

QUESTION #1: WHAT DO YOU USE ALL THE TIME?

I have to admit, I have an Amazon problem. It's not that I like wasting money buying senseless stuff—I tend to get a good deal of my household items from Amazon. Because of that, a lot of boxes come to my house. More than that, I need a way to open the myriad of boxes that come through my house, so my knife is something I use *all the time*, not just every now and again.

I use my keys all the time. I also need my wallet anytime I walk out of the house. My phone rarely leaves my side, whether I'm at home or not. I may not always wear my glasses, but they're always near me because I'm getting to the point where I can't always see things well without them.

I answer e-mails on my phone. I'm constantly listening to music, most often using my earbuds. I write a lot of notes, so I use pen and paper. I chew a lot of gum. These are some of things I use all the time.

Because I use these things all the time whether I'm at home or elsewhere, these should be a part of my EDC.

QUESTION #2: WHAT DO YOU USE SEVERAL TIMES A DAY?

Maybe you're a carpenter, and you carry a tool belt with a hammer, measuring tape, nails, screwdriver, and other tools. You use them all the time. But maybe several times a day, you use a pencil. It's probably something you should keep with you all the time, then. It would be a part of your EDC.

Do you use sunglasses anytime you're outside? Consider having a pair of sunglasses as a part of your EDC.

I know someone who gets food stuck in her teeth very easily. She uses floss several times a day.

I have a nail kit that I pull out at least once or twice a day—whether I tore a fingernail or have a hangnail.

I use lavender essential oil quite frequently.

I don't like to pull out my phone every time I want to know the time, so I use my watch multiple times every day. That should be a part of my EDC.

There are certain technology items that I will sometimes use multiple times a day, including my charger and charging cord.

What would you add to your list? What other items do you use multiple times a day?

QUESTION #3: WHAT DO YOU RUN INTO REGULARLY THAT YOU NEED TO DEAL WITH BETTER?

Now, maybe you have a kid who has a runny nose during cold and flu season. It would be so much easier and better if you had tissues with you. It doesn't matter if it's the nice pocket pack of tissues or even just a wad of tissues pulled from the box in your bedroom every morning.

Maybe you have a child who struggles with headaches. Make sure you always have Tylenol or Advil, or in our case, we need to have Arnica montana for our daughter, who gets migraines.

Or do you have a child who is just plain clumsy, one that is getting themselves scraped up all the time? Make sure that you have bandaids.

If I'm out, and I want to get an unsweetened iced tea, I always ask for lemon. If, however, the place I swing by doesn't have lemons, I want a lemon packet to use in place of it. I also like to carry several packets of Stevia sweetener for when I'm at a restaurant and they don't have Stevia.

For years, we had a child who would suffer from upset stomachs when we were on road trips. We learned to be proactive with peppermints and gallon-size zippered bags.

Are you a woman? You need to carry items with you for feminine emergencies.

Are you often on the go, but you're wanting to be careful of money? Maybe carrying a granola bar with you would be wise. Or if you need to have something that's protein-based, carrying meat sticks, like Slim Jims, would be more appropriate for you.

Do you ever end up in instances where you could use a flashlight? If so, it's time to start carrying one.

QUESTION #4: IF YOU COULDN'T LEAVE A LOCATION, WHAT WOULD YOU WANT TO HAVE WITH YOU?

If something happens and you can't leave a location, would you have everything that you need to deal with emergencies? These emergencies may be large or small.

If you have a nosebleed, running out to your car to get some tissues is impractical.

If you have an infant and you get stuck in a line, it's not always possible for you to leave your spot in line to run out to the car to get a toy or a snack for them. Even if you don't carry your diaper bag into a store, having a small toy or snack in the "purse" portion of your EDC is wise.

Another example of this would be when we were attacked by the young man with two knives while we were at chess club. It's not like I could have stood up and said, "Oh, just a second. I need to run out and get the pepper spray that I left in my car. I'll be right back!" You can't leave and get something in a situation like that.

What else could you add to this list?

QUESTION #5: WHAT ARE YOUR LIMITATIONS THAT YOU NEED TO WORK AROUND? AND WHAT ARE YOU GOING TO CARRY WITH YOU TO ADAPT TO THOSE LIMITATIONS?

This could be a physical limitation. At the moment, my oldest daughter carries an inhaler with her everywhere.

If you have a child who has dislocated their knee or sprained their ankle before, you may need to carry a knee brace or an ace wrap with you just in case.

Do you have diabetes? Do you need to carry hard candies or an "on-the-go" single-serving peanut butter cup and spoon with you in case your blood sugar goes low?

Do you get visual migraines? When I get these, I can't drive because I literally can't see. Carrying around caffeine, chocolate, and an essential-oil blend that I use for migraines helps alleviate at least the visual portion of the migraine in short order.

What limitations do you need to take into consideration, and what do you need to carry with you to mitigate them?

QUESTION #6: WHO AM I CARING FOR? WHAT ARE THEIR NEEDS?

Who am I caring for? This may sound like a "duh" type of question, but hang in there a moment. Yes, I have my kids with me much of the time, and occasionally my husband also comes along. Now, think outside of that. During the week, almost every time I go out during the day, my mom comes with me. Every Thursday evening, my mom, sister, and I go out. I may need to consider them as I'm planning my EDC.

Maybe you have a grandchild that lives near you that you take out on a regular basis. Maybe you care for an elderly neighbor and take him to run errands, or you babysit for a single mom. Take into consideration the people for whom you are caring, because that will inform what you carry in your EDC.

What are the needs of the people you bring with you? If you have your grandchild, depending on their needs, their mom may have a diaper bag for you, but it's also possible that there are special items you will want to carry as well. Work through these things.

QUESTION #7: WHAT FIRST AID ITEMS DO I NEED ON HAND "JUST IN CASE?"

First aid supplies are a simple way to make sure you're prepared. Start by asking yourself what first aid types of situations you often get into. Headaches? Scrapes? Burns? Allergies? Upset stomachs? And how do you plan on handling those things? What do you need on hand?

QUESTION #8: WHAT SURVIVAL ITEMS DO I NEED TO HAVE WITH ME "JUST IN CASE?"

I carry a lot of items with me that I use regularly. I'm out and I have a panic attack—lavender essential oil to the rescue. When I'm on the go and my nail breaks, I have clippers. When we eat at Chili's and corn on the cob gets stuck in my teeth, I have floss. What about items that we don't expect to need and nonetheless carry for emergencies?

What types of items would you wish you had with you if you were truly stuck?

Psst, while I'm having you work through these questions here, I'll be giving you suggestions at the end of the section one – Everyday Carry—not because I want you to go through and only use my suggestions, but because sometimes when we see a suggestion, we realize that there's value in it. So, while I want you to think through this section on your own, I will offer suggestions later in this section—especially when it comes to survival items.

QUESTION #9: FOR WHAT ITEM(S) DO I NEED TO BUILD A REDUNDANCY INTO MY EDC?

I have several children who enjoy borrowing (they would never steal) items from my EDC. At one point we were attending an evening Bible study at a friend's house and afterward, my children would go outside and play "Bear in the Night," which requires a flashlight. That's all well and good. The problem is that my flashlight doesn't always make it back into my backpack. Because of that, there are some things, like a flashlight, that I need to build in a redundancy for because otherwise, I might be without it when I need it.

Do your kids walk off with your fingernail clippers? Have you used up your tissues? Are you getting low on gum? Make sure that you have those necessary redundancies built in

Recap and Looking Ahead

So in this chapter, we've given you nine questions to formulate your family specific EDC. In the next chapter, we're going to discuss the seven categories that Everyday Carry falls into, and we'll dive into each. This will help you as you continue to grow your personalized list for your specific situation and family. Turn the page and let's jump into it!

Action Items:

1.) Get a piece of paper and a pen or pencil.
2.) Ask yourself the following questions and brainstorm items that you need:
    a. What do I use all the time?
    b. What do I use several times a day?
    c. What do I run into regularly that I need to deal with better?
    d. If I couldn't leave a location—what would I want with me?
    e. What are my limitations that I need to work around? What am I going to carry with me to adapt to those limitations?
    f. Who am I caring for? What are their needs?
    g. What first aid items do I need on hand "just in case?"

   h. What survival items do I need to have with me "just in case?"
   i. For what item(s) do I need to build redundancy into my EDC?

3.) Collate this into one list which will allow you to create your own EDC.

CHAPTER THREE

7 CATEGORIES OF EDC

"For every minute spent in organizing, an hour is earned."

— Benjamin Franklin

I have several friends who are EMTs or paramedics. When they go on a call, if they need to stabilize a patient before they reach the hospital, they have tools at their fingertips. If they need to start an IV, they know exactly where the equipment is—either in their pack or in the ambulance. If they need to stanch the flow of blood from a bad accident, they know where the tourniquets and absorbent materials are in their kit. If they need to check vitals, they can put their hands on exactly what they need at a moment's notice because their pack is organized.

Paramedics keep their ambulance and their pack organized, but not just as a randomized placement of items. They keep like items together. Their equipment for starting an IV is mostly going to be found in one place. The equipment for doing an EKG is all together. If there's an accident and they need to stop someone's bleeding, almost everything a paramedic needs is going to be kept together.

As we jump into our EDC categories, I want you to look at these the same way. If you have someone whose blood sugar is beginning to drop, you should have all the items you need for that occasion in one place. If your child has cut their finger, then everything you need to treat a minor cut should be kept together. That's why we're dealing with categories. When like items are categorized and organized together, we can find and get to them much more quickly and easily.

PHONE (AND OTHER ELECTRONICS)

We're going to start with the thing that the vast majority of people carry nowadays, whether or not you think about preparedness: our phone. It's usually in our back pocket, backpack, or even in our hand. The majority of us aren't going anywhere without our phone, and it's not just an item that keeps us connected or entertained. Let's talk about how our phones can be a powerful EDC tool.

Apps

I don't know about you, but when my kids think of phone apps, the first thing that comes to their mind is Spider Solitaire or Minion Rush or maybe Candy Crush. And yes, obviously, those are all apps. However, those are not tools—well, unless you count it as one because it's keeping a ten-year-old occupied during an unexpected delay or detour.

There are many apps you can add to your phone to turn it into a powerful tool. Let's briefly discuss some of them.

- **Flashlight Ruddy Rooster**. Normally, I wouldn't even suggest a flashlight app. I mean—why would you? Most phones have their own flashlights. If you're stuck and you need to get someone's attention, this app has a strobe feature. If you need to communicate with someone without using voice, it has a morse code feature! It has a hazard warning light feature. Not sure why you'd need it, but it also has a police light feature.

- **Open Signal**. There are various features on the Open Signal app, one of which is potentially really important during an emergency situation, and that is the Cell Tower Compass. If you find yourself stuck in an unfamiliar area and your cell phone isn't getting good reception, there's a cell tower compass that will tell you the direction of the nearest cell tower.
- **Zello**. This was the most downloaded app during Hurricane Harvey. It makes your cell phone useable as a walkie-talkie. Using Zello to send messages takes so much less bandwidth than a phone call. It will allow you to convey information to a pre-programmed network of friends and family by sending "blasts"—information that you need to get to the network you've already set up.
- **Offline Survival Manual**. You can download this app right from the Google Play store, but once it's downloaded, it's meant to be used totally offline, so if you're ever stuck in a survival situation, you can easily use its information.
- **Wiser**. Come in contact with a hazardous material? This app tells you what you should do and how you should handle the situation.
- **Red Cross First Aid**. Whether it's broken bones, bleeding, anaphylaxis, or a multitude of other occurrences, the Red Cross First Aid app will walk you through what to do step-by-step.
- **Weather Bug**. There are a multitude of weather apps. This just happens to be the one I use. I've also heard of another called Storm from the website Weather Underground.
- **PlantNet Plant Identification**. Need to know what plant you're looking at? This app will help identify it. This app has been invaluable on the farm that we purchased two years ago. You might not *think* that you need this app for preparedness, but if you want to know what the plant in front of you is and if it's edible. . . this app can help.

- **FM Radio app**. Need to hear a radio broadcast on your cell phone? You can use this app.
- **Reference Guide for Essential Oils**. If you're an essential oil aficionado, then this is the app for you. It will tell you which oils will work for various conditions and the way you should use them. Sorting by oils allows you to know what each is good for. This is a one-time purchase app.
- **FEMA**. This will allow you to put in zip codes for your loved ones, and once you do, it will let you know when that zip code has an alert—whether tornado, severe thunderstorm, or any other type of warning.
- **Useful Knots**. Need to know how to tie knots? This app will walk you through all types of knots and how to tie them step-by-step.
- **ICE**. The In Case of Emergency app will keep vital medical information available to first responders on your phone and lists out ICE information on your lock screen.
- **Amazon Kindle App**. Why in the world would I list this under preparedness tools? Because if you've purchased any survival Kindle books, you can download them to your phone and use them via this app.
- **Twitter**. Seriously! We lived in Ferguson, Missouri during the Ferguson Riots. When we needed to leave our house, we needed to know in which areas the rioting was taking place. For more than six months, there were protests of varying degrees of peacefulness going on almost 24/7. I could get on Twitter, search #Ferguson, and see where people were at that exact moment. We needed to know in order to keep our family safe.

When phones can't be used as phones

Sometimes we need to communicate with people, but our phones can't or won't function as regular communication devices. This might be because of a natural disaster taking out cell phone towers. This might be because too many people are trying to use the network all at once. This might be because you're stuck in a part of a building with bad cell reception.

How do you get around this type of problem if you really *do* need to communicate with the outside world? There are several ways you can let people know all is well.

Out of area contact

Why is it sometimes impossible to get a local phone call to go through—especially during an emergency? Because it takes *two* connections in the area—yours and theirs—in order for the phone call to go through.

So, if you have family or close friends in your area whom you want to check on, there is a better way. Everyone *in* your area you want to communicate with should have the name and phone number of a person *outside* of your calling area. Here's why: If you call someone outside of your area, you're only tying up one local circuit. If there's a natural disaster and you need to communicate, you can each call that out-of-area contact and provide them with information to pass along as others call.

For us, everyone in our family who has a phone knows that if they aren't able to reach us because the circuits are full, they are to call my father-in-law in Texas. My mom could call my father-in-law and let him know that she's okay. My sister could call my father-in-law, and then she would hear that Mom is okay and would let Ron, my father-in-law, know that she's also okay. Then when we're able to, we would call him as well and he would let us know that everyone who has already called is safe.

Make sure that all your family and close friends in your area have the name and phone number for the same person outside of your area. Then make sure they know that they are to call in case of a local emergency.

Various types of texting

Regular texting. Even if you can't make a phone call, try texting. Those will often send and receive even when calls can't go through.

Facebook. If you can't get a text through, leave a message on Facebook. Facebook also has an excellent feature where you can "Mark yourself safe during. . ." and it lists an event. This is a great way to let out-of-area people, as well as family who are in different locations, know that you're safe.

Twitter. You can send out a tweet to let friends know that you're safe.

Discord. You can change your personal status on Discord to reflect that you're safe.

Change your phone message

Another less conventional way to let people know you're okay is to change your phone's message. You can change your message to let people know that you're safe, or where you are in the case of a disaster if you feel people may be looking for you. This way, even if you can't receive a call, the people trying to reach you will find out that you're okay.

Phone accessories

If you're going to carry your phone with you, please don't forget your phone accessories.

These would include an extra battery bank and a charging cord that allows you to charge your phone.

You likely also need earbuds with a mic for two reasons. If there's a lot of yelling going on around you, you aren't going to hear well unless you have earbuds. But the reason that earbuds with a mic are important is if you're out doing something with your hands, walking, running, or trying to help someone, you can listen to the person on the other end of your phone *and* you can talk hands-free.

SANITATION AND HYGIENE

You might think, gee whiz—apart from carrying a pad and a tampon with me, what more do I really need for sanitation and hygiene?

It's interesting, this is the category I most reach for in my backpack. If my hands are dry, and we're out, I'll want to put some lotion on them. Well, I keep lotion in my hygiene bag. It might be that my lips are chapped, so I pull out some lip balm. It could be that we're at church and one of my kids has forgotten to comb their hair and it's sticking out all kinds of crazy directions. Of course, I only noticed once we arrived. I can hand them a comb and send them to the bathroom. My girls have accidentally broken ponytail holders while we're out. I keep an extra in my hygiene bag. I have a child who likes to pull hangnails all-the-stinking-time. I keep nail clippers so I can clip them before he pulls them (if he tells me about them). Even things like keeping powder, tissues, or an eyeglass repair kit—and yes, absolutely a pad and a tampon—are vital parts of my hygiene kit. I also keep sunscreen, a small, really sharp pair of scissors, a yarn needle, a hair clip, bobby pins, hand sanitizer, and floss. Floss is extra cool because it can also work as cordage and is pretty strong for its size.

So, when it comes to all things hygiene, think travel-size—not full-size—options. Other things you may want to keep in this bag are travel powder, bug spray, and wet wipes or baby wipes.

HEALTH AND FIRST AID

I keep two different containers with health items in them. One of the things that I keep is a pill minder. If you don't know what a pill minder is, it's a container that has seven mini sections in it—one (or two depending on the pill minder) for each day of the week. I have a different use for these.

In the pill minder I keep in my backpack, I keep different items in each of the individual sections, including: two pairs of nitrile gloves, twenty Advil, twenty Tylenol, Bayer aspirin, Band-Aids, Benadryl, and Advil PM. This way I keep most of the pills we might need while we're out and about in one easy location. They're all together and well-organized. I can access them easily without having to carry those itty-bitty pouches that have only two pills. And remembering to replace a pouch can easily fall through the cracks. Not having medicines when I or a loved one is in pain should be a moot point.

That's the first part of my health and first aid EDC—then there's part two. In this part, I carry a bandana which can be used as a tourniquet, sling, or even as a makeshift dust mask. I carry "Neo To Go!" I also carry a partial ace wrap. It's only a part of one because an entire ace wrap would be too bulky. To do this, get an ace wrap, cut a section off, and fasten it with a safety pin. It's enough to wrap ankles, wrists, elbows, or even knees. It will provide some support until you can get back home to your first aid supplies. I also have medical tape, wound seal, Arnica, superglue, Benadryl spray, and steri strips. I can take care of pretty much any small first aid emergency when we're not at home with the first aid category of my EDC.

FOOD AND HYDRATION

The next category of items is food and hydration. In this category, I carry mints and hard candies for several reasons. Did you know that a regular old peppermint can help someone whose stomach is upset? We use them on trips for our son who gets motion sick. We also carry hard candies because I have a daughter whose blood sugar gets low, and hard candies help bring her blood sugar up faster than a snack could.

I carry a protein bar so that if I have to miss a meal, I won't worry about being hungry for too long.

I keep a drink mix packet so if I haven't eaten yet, but I need to get some hydration (or take a pill), I can add the drink mix to a water bottle. I've mentioned that if I drink water on an empty stomach, it gets upset. I prefer iced tea mix packets, but there are other options. I've seen lemonade, cherry, grape, and even orange drink mixes. No, they aren't the healthiest, but they do serve a purpose. And if you have kids in sports, you might want to consider carrying Gatorade's drink mixes. These mixes are various flavors and contain electrolytes to help with dehydration.

The last thing I carry with me is a water bottle. This is typically in my car kit. We do have Berkey water bottles that we keep in our vehicle, but if I know I'm going for a walk or going to be away from home for a while, I'll bring a water bottle.

GENERAL PREPAREDNESS/SURVIVAL

Some of you are probably thinking, "Well Karen, all of this is preparedness." Yes, it is, but there are some things that fall into the category of preparedness more squarely than general hygiene supplies.

So, what do I mean by "general preparedness/survival?" If I were stuck on my own in the middle of nowhere – what is the basic minimum of supplies I would need to survive? If an item affirmatively answers that question – it belongs in this category. The first item I carry in this category of my EDC is a way to start a fire. I actually carry four ways to start a fire: an arc lighter (and no, I don't smoke), waterproof matches, a small magnifying glass, and a flint (which I can use with my knife to start a fire).

Another item to consider is a length of duct tape. When I kept a cigarette lighter instead of an arc lighter, I wrapped the tape around the cigarette lighter. Now, I use an empty lip balm container to wrap the tape around. Duct tape is handy in many different ways for many different things, but why keep it around a huge cardboard tube? This saves so much space if I wrap it around something I'm already carrying.

I also keep extra-heavy-duty bootlaces. Why bootlaces? If my shoelace breaks, I have one that I don't have to worry about breaking again easily. Will those khaki-colored laces look a little weird on my white tennis shoes? Maybe, but will they work and hold together well? Absolutely. I also carry bootlaces because my husband and son almost exclusively wear boots. This is another example of customizing my EDC for my family. It might look different for yours. Besides allowing you to replace broken shoelaces or bootlaces, these also give you cordage. If you need to tie something down, heavy-duty bootlaces will work very well.

Finally, I keep a mirror, whistle, strong flashlight, and a compass in this section of my kit. These are the items that allow me to take care of basic needs if I were stranded while away from home.

PROTECTION

When we were caught in the library during chess club by the young man with a knife, I realized just how unprepared I was for something of that magnitude. I knew I couldn't carry a gun (even with a concealed carry permit) into our library, so I needed to seek other avenues that would allow me to better protect my family. One of the first things I did was to purchase pepper spray. Now, pepper spray isn't legal to carry everywhere. You need to check out your local laws before you go purchase some from Amazon. However, pepper spray is a great way to keep you safe because it blinds your attacker and makes it hard for him or her to breathe, giving you sufficient time to get away.

Besides mace or pepper spray, your phone is another avenue you can use for protection. When we were attacked, I didn't think of my phone as a preparedness item. I could have called 911 from inside the room and let them listen to what was going on—our coach was talking very loudly to the young man. The police would have picked up on at least some of what was going on even if I couldn't talk.

There's an article on my blog about different types of protection you can use, and someone left a message saying I had forgotten our most easily accessible way of protecting ourselves: our voice. If you're walking outside and see someone following you, screaming is an appropriate method of calling attention to yourself. If you're near your vehicle and it has a car alarm, you could hit the alarm button.

Other ways you can protect yourself include carrying a pocketknife, or if you have a concealed carry permit, you can carry your firearm. If you do concealed or open carry, make sure to carry an extra mag with you.

Other, less lethal options would be something like a stun gun, but again, check the laws for your area, as they aren't legal in all places.

FAMILY-SPECIFIC

Every family is going to be different. My daughter carries an inhaler. My mother is diabetic. My son gets car sick on long trips. I have another daughter who's prone to headaches.

If you have a baby, you're probably used to carrying a diaper bag with you. Have you considered how devastated a slightly older child with a "lovie" might be if separated from that animal even for one night? At one point, my son carried his Pooh Bear around with him everywhere! I bought an identical Pooh and kept it with me so that if for some reason we couldn't get home and he lost it, I would have one with me.

Do you often find yourself having to wait for people? Make sure you have extra books downloaded on your phone so you have something to do. Or have a game or two downloaded. You could even carry cards with you and play a card game. There are many different card games you can play "solitaire" style. My family loves to play Dutch Blitz and Phase 10; these are both very easily carried in my EDC bag. I carry two decks of playing cards with me so that if we're out and

I want to pass some time either by myself or with my kids, we have card games we know and love.

Your family-specific items will likely fall under one of the other six categories—which is fine, but I do want you to think through the things that serve your family's unique needs.

Recap and Looking Ahead

In this chapter, we've discussed seven categories of EDC. We've delineated what types of items fall into each category, and we've walked through how to develop your own EDC to fit your own needs.

In the next chapter, we're going to talk about how to use our EDC. How do you organize your EDC so that you know where everything is and you can put your finger on anything at a moment's notice? How do you determine if your EDC is still serving you? From time to time we go through and do a thorough review of what we're carrying to make sure we're working efficiently. We'll discuss how to know if you're in need of upgrading any of your EDC items. Then finally, we'll talk through how to go about training with your EDC so that you are able to use that pepper spray if, heaven forbid, you ever need it. So turn the page, and let's dive into the nitty gritty of using your EDC effectively.

Action Items:

1.) Take a piece of regular-sized paper. Fold it in half both long-ways and short-ways. This gives you eight sections—four on the front, and four on the back. Label each section with one category of EDC.
2.) Do you currently have an EDC? Great! Inventory your items on your list.
3.) If you don't have a planned EDC, everyone carries something with them each day. Even if you just have your

purse or your pockets. Inventory those items so that you know exactly what you have with you. It's easy to assume that because you had that comb in your bag last week, it's still there.

4.) Return to your EDC list from chapter two. Go through your house and gather the items that you already have, but are not already a part of your EDC.
5.) For items that you don't already have and want to purchase, prioritize the list and decide which item is the most important, then the second most important, and so on.
6.) Designate an out-of-area contact person (with their permission) and disseminate his or her phone number to all your family and close friends in the area. Explain how and when to use that contact person.

CHAPTER FOUR

EDC ORGANIZATION, REVIEW, UPGRADE, AND TRAINING

> "There is only one kind of shock worse than the totally unexpected: the expected for which one has refused to prepare."
>
> — Mary Renault

There are some things that cannot be foreseen. When we went to chess club for the second time, how in the world were we supposed to know that a young man would come running into the room brandishing two knives and threatening to kill us all? Nothing could have taken any of us more by surprise. But I can guarantee you that if we get into a car and my middle son decides (unwisely) to read a book or focus on his Kindle, his stomach is going to get upset. Take it to the bank. I wish I had been more prepared for the first scenario, but there's no excuse for me not to be prepared for the second scenario. That is what EDC is for. We are preplanning for emergencies we can anticipate and working to plan for emergencies we cannot.

Using your EDC might seem like a common sense thing that doesn't need addressing, but we're going to break down how to use your EDC into several categories: EDC Organization, Review, Upgrade, and Training. Let's jump in with EDC Organization.

EDC ORGANIZATION

When you're doing EDC properly, it's very well organized. You know where everything is. You know what you need, and where you can find it. Great organization allows you to help people as quickly as possible.

A group from church had gone over to help someone new in the area clean out their newly purchased house. While the adults were inside cleaning this house that had been vacant for a while, the kids were doing exactly what kids do—playing. Some of the kids were playing tag in the backyard where there was a chain-link fence. One kid's feet slipped underneath and when he pulled it back, he cut his foot. Because I knew exactly which pouch in my backpack was for first aid, I could grab it quickly. I didn't have to look through each one. I didn't have to guess. I wasn't worried that I couldn't find it. Because it's easily organized, it means that your items are quickly out so that you can deal with whatever the problem is as quickly as possible.

Having all of these things in your purse or backpack is wonderful, but if you have to literally turn your backpack upside down and empty it of all its contents to find something, you're going to be in a world of hurt.

Practical Principles

When I first organized my EDC, I headed out to the Dollar Store to purchase cosmetic bags. More recently, I ordered some inexpensive cosmetic bags from Amazon to replace the old ones. Make sure to have at least six (if not seven) cosmetic bags with different prints. The different print is very important— it's how you'll identify which bag contains which items quickly.

I put each category in a different makeup bag. All my bags are the same size: 8" long, 5" tall, and 2" deep, and all have a different print. My navy-blue striped bag holds my hygiene items. My red striped bag holds my first aid items. My pink striped bag holds my food and drink items. My khaki striped bag holds my survival items. I keep them all in my backpack.

For you guys out there, I went to Amazon and searched, "masculine make-up style bags," and found a set of "travel cubes" that are fairly small and would work well. The entire set of seven bags cost around $16. So there's a way that you can do this, too.

I do keep a few things in my backpack which are not in a makeup bag. One is a preparedness kit from Amazon which is about 6"x4"x2". It has a space blanket, a pocket chainsaw, a flint and steel, flashlight, survival pen, compass, whistle, credit card multitool, small knife, and a paracord bracelet. I also carry some essential oils in a slot in my backpack so that I know exactly where they are. I carry pens and pencils in their designated slots as well as a small notebook called a "Little Fat Book" so I can take notes or have paper for kindling. I keep an extra set of keys because I used to lock myself out of my car on a regular basis. There is also a specific pocket on my backpack that I use for my computer and phone supplies.

EDC REVIEW

We all change. Our roles change. The seasons change. Our needs change. Our wants change. Even our tastes change. So, when it comes to our ECD, it's natural that it will forever be in flux. Once or twice a year, you should spend time reviewing your EDC.

Again, we're going to tackle this review by asking some questions. (1) What is working well for you? (2) What is working for you, but only marginally? (3) What isn't working for you at all? (4) What item(s) are you always looking for, but never have? (5) What item(s) do you never use, and can't ever imagine using?

1.) What is working well for you?

When you begin reviewing your EDC, ask yourself: what is working well?

- Do you love the size, weight, or look of your bag?
- How about your flashlight—has it ceased to "wow" you with its usefulness and power?
- Are you always reaching for a bar of some sort because you're out and about in need of a snack so you don't hit fast food *again*? And you always have a bar in your bag?
- Do you not have babies anymore, but you find that you're always pulling wipes or Wet Ones out, and you're so glad to have them?
- Are you always ready with an adhesive bandage, and do your kids need them a lot?

What is working for you? It could be these things—but more than likely there's something that struck you as soon as I asked the question. It's that one thing that you always sigh with relief over because you need it again, and you know you have it. You need to take note of this, because you want to make sure that when you adjust other items in your bag, you don't somehow undo this good thing.

2.) What is working for you, but only marginally?

We all have it. That item you're glad you have, but it isn't working as well for you as you anticipated it would. Maybe it's a pair of fingernail clippers? You're thankful you have them, but they don't seem to be sharp enough. Maybe you like your wet wipes, but the brand you've been using seems to dry out too soon. Perhaps the lip balm you keep in your bag melts easily in the summer. Maybe the type of bar that you carry in your bag has satisfied your hunger, but it leaves your stomach feeling a bit off.

Each of these things work, and you're glad you have them, but something about them doesn't work as well as it should, and definitely not as well as it could. You need to take note of this and make slight tweaks. If your fingernail clippers are not sharp enough, replace them. If your wet wipes dry out too quickly, look for another brand. Your lip balm melts in the summer? Look for another brand that stays hard even in the heat of the summer. If your granola or protein bar leaves your stomach upset, try other kinds to see which type sits best in your system.

You get the idea. You may like the concept of having a certain item in your bag, but that particular type of item doesn't work for you. Find a better item. Hopefully, you'll take those items from being ones that work only marginally well to ones that work amazingly!

3.) What isn't working for you at all?

Is there something about your EDC that isn't working at all? Do you always feel on edge when you're carrying a firearm? Does your bag, backpack, or purse chafe your shoulders? Does it just not fit you right? Do you carry steri-strips as a part of your first aid kit, but they come apart from the paper and get stuck to everything else? Every time you walk out the door, do you hesitate before picking up your bag because it's just too heavy? When you practice with your EDC firearm, is there a particular clip that keeps giving you fits?

There are so many things that could go wrong with your EDC. Yet despite that fact, sometimes we just ignore things that aren't working because we're too fixated on the fact that we have "stuff" just in case we need it.

As you review your EDC, this is the perfect time to make changes. If something specific isn't working for you, it doesn't mean you need to ditch the item all together. If your bag is badly chafing your shoulders—ask yourself why. Is your bag not a good fit for your frame? Maybe the bag is poorly constructed and something in that poor construction digs into your shoulders or side when you carry it. Is it too heavy because you tried to cram in too much stuff? Don't just get rid of the bag, evaluate what isn't working.

If it's a poorly constructed bag, go out and try on other bags. See which ones feel best on your shoulders. Are you a woman who wears size 2x? You need a different bag than someone who wears a size medium. Different bags are built for different people. Find *your* bag.

4.) What items are you always looking for, but never have?

When anyone gives recommendations for items to include in your bag—whether me or anyone else— you need to remember that those recommendations are based on us and what we know. You live a totally different life and may have totally different needs.

We all have at least one item that makes us think, "Oh, I really could use. . . right now!" You need to add that item to an EDC list. If you didn't start a list at the end of chapter two, start one now. If you can't start one on paper this second, e-mail it to yourself, and don't delete the e-mail until you've created a list and put that item on your EDC list.

Do you find yourself waiting for your kids at piano lessons, and you feel like you're just wasting time by playing games on your phone? Slip a small book into your bag. Maybe your stomach gets upset easily, but you don't carry anything with you to help combat it. Add your stomach-aid of choice to your list.

Several times, I've found myself out and end up in a deluge of rain. I decided that having a mini umbrella in my bag was worth the investment.

Recently, we got outdoor cats to help deal with our mouse problem. We can't have them inside because we have one child who is very allergic and another who is mildly allergic. One of my allergic children still loves to pick them up and love on them. It's a domino effect. He loves the cats, so he picks them up.

Because he picks them up, his nose runs. When his nose runs, he licks his lips *a lot*. Licking his makes them chapped. I had recently gone through and pared down my EDC and removed my lip balm because I never used it. But now—you guessed it. I put it back in because my son needs it almost every day.

5.) What items do you never use, and can never imagine using?

We all have them. I know when I first started creating my EDC I used other people's lists to help me decide what to carry. I have a friend who swears that carrying an Israeli tourniquet is absolutely necessary. Now I do keep one in my comprehensive first aid kit that comes with us on long trips, but I see no need to carry one with me all the time. I have bandanas and pencils in my "preparedness" mini bag. One bandana with a pencil can create a tourniquet in a pinch, and I can use items that I already have or can easily find—this keeps clutter out of my bag.

Which are those items for you? Which items do you not need or can repurpose other supplies to do just as well.

PARING DOWN YOUR BAG

I have a regular-sized adult backpack that I got from Lands' End when their backpacks were better quality. It is strong, sturdy, and has a lot of nooks and crannies for my stuff. The shoulders are well padded and there's a clip that goes across my chest so the straps won't fall off my shoulders. It is wonderful. But as my needs (and concerns) grew, I started carrying more and more in my backpack. It got to the point that I didn't want to carry it around with me. It was just too heavy. If you find yourself in this situation, you may need to pare down your backpack's contents. Let me walk you through the process I used.

Go back to your seven questions in chapter two. What do I *really* have to have? Go through each category separately. Maybe you've put together a bag based solely on someone's recommendations and as you go back through your hygiene bag, you realize, "Ya know—I've never used powder in my life, let alone when I'm away from home. Why in the world am I carrying this?" Remember :this is your bag. Not my bag. This is not some male prepper gurus's bag. You need to customize it for you. Maybe you've never found yourself in a situation where you need sunblock. Take it out! Customize your bag for you!

Say you're a guy and you keep your hair buzzed, you don't need a comb! Remember your layers. Remember there are times when you're just going to have what's in your pockets. There are times when you may just have what's in your pockets and in your small purse, or for guys that MOLLE bag. You don't have to carry every single layer with you all the time! In almost every situation, as long as you have what you need to protect yourself, you should be fine. You should be able to get out to your car or to your backpack.

If you're carrying too much, utilize the layers. My backpack is still a smidge too heavy to want to carry it with me all the time. Most times now, it stays in my vehicle and I have my most pressing necessities in my purse.

WHEN TO GIVE YOUR EDC AN UPGRADE

Your EDC review and your EDC upgrade are integral. In many cases you can't do an EDC upgrade unless you've done an EDC review (whether planned or impromptu). Your upgrade will, out of necessity, be based on your review. So, under what circumstances should you consider an EDC upgrade?

Are you out of something?

Sometimes there are items in my EDC I run out of. I carry different varieties of hard candy that need to be replaced from time to time. I've had to replace Band-Aids because I run out of them. We've used up floss, different types of food bars, first aid wrap, gum, and so many other things.

When you do this, it's a great time to ask yourself—are you satisfied with what you had, or should you upgrade to a better version of the item? I've discovered that I really appreciate sturdy cloth Band-Aids much more than plastic Band-Aids. So, when I ran out of plastic Band-Aids, I decided to replace them with sturdy cloth ones.

I found a lotion from Bath and Body Works that I love because it's in a long, skinny tube, and I can easily fit it into my EDC makeup bag. So even if I run out of that lotion, I won't go and look for another. I know what I like and am well served by the one I've chosen.

Have you lost something?

Inevitably it happens: I'm out running errands, and I need to jot a note on a piece of paper. I dig into my backpack for my pen—only to remember that during church last week, my daughter asked to borrow my pen to take notes and never gave it back. And it's not just pens. My flashlights often turn up missing, whether because the kids were playing a game and wanted it or because they wanted to go looking for something under a bed, etc.

Is there an item that doesn't work how you want it to?

I can't tell you how many kinds of flashlights I purchased before I settled on one specific flashlight that I loved. I've had small keychain flashlights that would easily fall off. I've had flashlights that were not nearly as bright as I needed them to be. I've had flashlights that broke easily and wouldn't turn on. I've had flashlights whose coverage area was just too small. So each time I bought a flashlight, I tried to upgrade to a slightly better one. Usually, something about each was a bit off or presented me with new challenges. So when I found a flashlight that was lightweight, had a powerful light, enough coverage, and didn't easily break—I stuck with it.

Don't be afraid to experiment with your EDC until you find what works perfectly for you!

Do you need to add to your EDC?

You don't know what you don't know. It's an oft used phrase to point out that we can't know a fact until we are introduced to it. The same holds true of our equipment. We may need something in our EDC, but we don't understand that need until someone points out a hole in our equipment plans or shows us a new gadget that will fill a hole of which we were unaware. This section is geared toward helping you determine if you need to add a new type of item to your EDC or if you need to replace an item in your EDC with something more targeted to meet your individual needs.

Most of us have had one of these moments. One of our friends wants to show off a new gadget they got and they fawn over its features, craftsmanship, and uses. By the time they're done, you don't just want one; you see the real value of having one.

From the start, make sure you do your research. Maybe the one that they have is decent, but when you check it out on a website that does reviews of that particular item, you find out that there's one with better reviews which doesn't cost considerably more. Make sure you're taking your time to find the right item for you.

Upgrade/replacement quality

Let's talk for a moment about the quality of the upgrade. If you already have your EDC filled out and you're merely upgrading one or two items, that's a different scenario than if you're building out your entire EDC. If you already have the vast majority of what you need and want for your EDC, I would encourage you to upgrade with the best that you can afford. Why?

In the last year, I was introduced to a series of books written by Terry Pratchett set in a place called "Discworld." Normally, while fun to read, I wouldn't tout them as having incredible real-world examples and experiences to draw from. But in this instance, I think something that Sir Terry talks about hits the nail on the head.

Pratchett explains the reason we should spend a little extra to invest in quality items this way:

> "The reason that the rich were so rich, Vimes reasoned, was because they managed to spend less money. Take boots, for example. He earned thirty-eight dollars a month plus allowances. A really good pair of leather boots cost fifty dollars. But an affordable pair of boots, which were sort of OK for a season or two and then leaked … when the cardboard gave out, cost about ten dollars. Those were the kind of boots Vimes always bought, and wore until the soles were so thin that he could tell where he was in Ankh- Morpork on a foggy night by the feel of the cobbles. But the thing was that good boots lasted for years and years. A man who could afford fifty dollars had a pair of boots that'd still be keeping his feet dry in ten years' time, while the poor man who could only afford cheap boots would have spent a hundred dollars on boots in the same time and

> *would still have wet feet.*" Terry Pratchett – *Men at Arms*

And Pratchett is right: by spending a little more up front, you end up spending less overall. I find this is so very true—not only with footwear, but with clothing in general. I can go to Walmart and purchase a $20 pair of blue jeans. That pair of blue jeans is much cheaper than buying a pair of blue jeans at say, Lane Bryant. But what I've found is that if I get a pair of blue jeans on sale at Lane Bryant and pay double the cost of the Walmart blue jeans, I still come out ahead because Lane Bryant blue jeans last more than twice as long as the Walmart ones.

The principle holds true in almost every area of life. Most of the time—unless it's an immediate need that we can't wait on—we almost always end up saving up and purchasing one of the more expensive models of whatever it is we're looking at because we don't want to have to replace it sooner.

EDC TRAINING

I can hear some of you now: "Karen, it's just a flashlight. Why in the world do I need to train with my flashlight?" Well, there are some items in our EDC that we definitely don't need to take time to make sure we're using the most efficiently. However, there are several items that I'd like to discuss the benefits of being trained in.

The most obvious one being. . .

Do you concealed or open carry?

If you carry a firearm, you need to know how to use it. You need to know what to do if that firearm doesn't perform as it's supposed to. You need to be able to take that firearm apart, clean it, and put it back together again. You need to practice with your firearm for accuracy. You need to feel comfortable handling that firearm, and that won't happen unless you've trained.

Do you carry pepper spray or mace?

One night when I was out walking my dog before we moved to the farm, another dog started following us. First, it just walked behind us. Then it began barking at us. Then it began low growling at us. At that point, I picked up my little dog (a dachshund/Yorkshire terrier mix), but the dog kept coming.

Fortunately for me, I had pepper spray and I used it on the dog. But when I pulled it out to use it, I

realized that I had never used it before, and really didn't know what I was doing with it. After that incident, I began to practice using my pepper spray. If you have daughters who carry pepper spray or mace, they should also practice.

How far does it shoot? Does it shoot in a single stream, a fanned-out spray, or as more of an aerosol? Are you going to be affected by spraying it? I have a daughter for whom that might be an issue. You need to know these things before you need to use it.

Do you carry an arc lighter?

An arc lighter is like a cigarette lighter in that you can use it to light a fire. However, an arc lighter creates an electric current, not a flame. The electric current will set flammable materials on fire, but do you know how to use it? Do you know how close to get it to the material? Did you even know that you need to charge your arc lighter?

Practice with your items. Have you tried using your waterproof matches? Are you aware that they're waterproof because the tip of the match is covered in a wax-like material? Have you ever tried striking one to use it? How many strikes does it take to remove the wax-like material?

Does your flashlight have different settings? Can it strobe? Does it have intensity settings? Do you have to charge it? Have you checked its batteries lately (if there are any)? All of these are things that you should work through and train with—not just *have* them in your EDC.

Recap and Looking Ahead

In this chapter, we've covered many different facets of how to use EDC. We discussed EDC Organization, Review, Upgrade, and even Training.

In the next chapter, Helping Others with EDC and Vehicle Preparedness, we're going to discuss the – nearly effortless – way that you can help other moms find levels of preparedness that they are wanting, but aren't sure how to go about obtaining. So flip the page, and let's dive in.

Action Items:

1.) Look at your local dollar store or on Amazon for cosmetic bags in which to organize your EDC. Make sure that all of the bags are unique so that everything is easy to find.
2.) If you have an already developed EDC, do a review.
    a. What is working well? Let's keep that.
    b. What is working marginally? Should you replace that?
    c. What isn't working at all? Do you need it? If so, with what should you replace it?
    d. What are you looking for, but never have? Should you add it?
    e. What do you have in your bag, but you can never see yourself using? Should you get rid of it?
3.) Consider whether you are in need of an EDC Upgrade.
    a. Are you out of an item like lotion? Do you want the same kind or would you like to look for another that will better fit your needs?

b. Have you lost an item? Do you want to purchase the exact same item? Is there one that will better equip you at a similar price?
c. Do you have an item that you use, but this particular version isn't working for you? Should you replace it with one that has the features for which you are looking?

4.) Go through each items in your EDC and make sure that you know how to use them properly, safely, and effectively – especially items such as: a firearm, a taser, mace / pepper spray, arc lighter, P-51 can opener, your pocket knife, etc.

CHAPTER FIVE

HELPING OTHERS WITH EDC AND VEHICLE PREPAREDNESS

> "People who help others (with zero expectation) experience higher levels of fulfillment, live longer, and make more money."
>
> —Alex Hormozi

I used to live on one of the busiest street corners in Ferguson, Missouri. This location had both advantages and disadvantages; hence, one of the things that I often noticed was the numerous knocks that I'd get on my door. I'd get requests for a sandwich, for work, or to be driven somewhere. As often as I could, I would accommodate these entreaties.

But why would I do that? I didn't garner anything from it. I gained no money, no accolades, and sometimes even no thanks. Honestly, though I didn't do it to feel good,but I *did* feel good. It felt good to help someone who I had never met before.

If you were given that same opportunity – to do good to someone that you'd never met - would you take it? What if it took you no money and less than sixty seconds? Would you do it?

The only way that we, at "Are You Prepared, Mama?," can accomplish our goal of helping every mom better care for her family in good times and bad, is if preparedness-minded moms know we're here to help.

Out there somewhere is someone who really needs this book. There is a mom who feels like she's always behind the eight-ball and unable to get ahead of the ongoing little challenges that life is constantly throwing at her. And in her own mind, if she is struggling to handle the little challenges, how is she going to deal with the more substantial ones? What if – for no money - you could give that mom hope? What if you could encourage her with the certainty that there are some little things she can do right now that require very little time and no money. More than that, doing these little things would immediately relieve some of the pressure she's feeling? Would you do it? Would you help her?

Maybe you're wondering how you could help that mom. The answer is very simple. Let's face it. Most people judge a book by its cover and its reviews. Every review that is left on this book is a signpost to one or more moms who need this book. Don't tell *the world* that they can gain more control over their circumstances. Just tell one mom through a review. Don't tell the whole world that they can protect their family from unexpected calamities - big or small. Just tell *one mom* by leaving an Amazon review.

If this book has inspired, encouraged, motivated, and/or informed you, would you please take just a couple of moments to leave an honest review of this book?

Your review will help ...

... bring hope to the mom who is stuck under the never-ending cycle of carpool, permission slips and soccer practices.

... instruct the mom who knows she wants to do more but isn't sure of the next step.

... encourage the mom who feels isolated on her quest to help her family prepare for life's unexpected emergencies. She'll finally grasp that she's not alone in her struggles.

... comfort the mom who thinks she is so far behind that there is no use attempting to better her situation. You'll show her that she's probably not as far behind as she thinks and that she can make real headway faster than she believes.

All it takes to provide hope and help to preparedness-minded moms - and this takes less than 60 seconds - is for you to leave a review.

- If you are reading this on Kindle or Kindle reader for your phone, double tap any page. This will give you a location indicator at the bottom of the page. Move that indicator to the end of the book, tap once on the last page, and then swipe up. That will allow you to leave a review.
- When it's available, if you are listening on Audible, click the three dots in the top right-hand corner and then select "Rate and Review" on the pop-up menu.
- If you purchased the paperback, go to Amazon.com in your web browser, and search for the title Mom on the Run in books. Then scroll to the bottom of the page and leave a review.

If you took some time to leave a review, you are my kind of person, and because you were willing to help a mom that you've never met before, I want to help you. I have a Facebook Membership Group called "A Year Without the Grocery Store Workbook Group." Go to Facebook and search for that group. Request to be admitted, and let the administrator know you left a review for Mom on the Run. In the group you'll find challenges to move your preparedness forward, extra preparedness content not released anywhere else, encouragement when things are going right, and answers when things aren't going as planned.

I do what I do so that I can bless others. Thank you for giving me that opportunity to bless you and other moms.

Recap and Looking Ahead

In this chapter, we've discussed the benefits of helping others with preparedness.

In the addendum to this section, you'll find my EDC recommendations. After that, you're finished with the first section of this guide. But don't stop there! We've got a whole section in this book devoted to being prepared when you are in your vehicle. You'll learn how to take care of emergencies that would outstrip what you have in your EDC. You'll learn what additional items you may need to add to your vehicle beyond what's in your EDC. We'll discuss how to organize your items, how to fit all of your items into your car and so much more! So keep flipping those pages and join me in Section Two – The Prepared Vehicle.

SECTION ONE: EVERYDAY CARRY

ADDENDUM

EDC Checklist

> "Organizing is what you do before you do something so that when you do it, it is not all mixed up."
>
> — A. A. Milne

Now—and only now that you've walked through how to choose proper items for your EDC—I want to take you through my EDC lists. *Not* because I want you to copy my list—please, please don't. But I want to encourage you to think through things, and maybe this list will cause you to think of something you might have otherwise missed.

Phone and Electronics

- ○ Phone
- ○ Ear buds
- ○ Charging cord
- ○ Phone charger

Food and Drink

- ○ Gum
- ○ Granola bars or single-serve granola packets
- ○ Lemon packets
- ○ Mints
- ○ Hard candies
- ○ Meat sticks

First Aid Supplies

- ○ Band-Aids – various sizes
- ○ Butterfly closures
- ○ Neosporin
- ○ Adhesive wrap
- ○ Alcohol wipes
- ○ Tylenol
- ○ Advil
- ○ Benadryl
- ○ Advil PM
- ○ Aspirin
- ○ Benadryl spray
- ○ Gloves
- ○ Bandana
- ○ Wound seal
- ○ Nosebleed stop
- ○ Super glue
- ○ Cough drops

Preparedness Tools

- ○ Arc lighter
- ○ Flashlight
- ○ Waterproof matches
- ○ Duct tape – I wrap mine around a cigarette lighter or an empty tube of lip balm
- ○ Knife
- ○ Multitool
- ○ Mirror – for signaling
- ○ Bootlaces
- ○ Headlamp
- ○ Magnesium rod
- ○ Magnifying glass
- ○ Compass
- ○ Space blanket
- ○ Hand-pull chainsaw
- ○ Paracord bracelet
- ○ Pocket knife

Sanitation

- ○ Go-Girl
- ○ Fingernail kit – so many helpful tools beyond fingernail clippers
- ○ Wet wipes
- ○ Hand lotion
- ○ Lip balm
- ○ Hair ties
- ○ Comb

- Bobby pins
- Hair clips
- Floss
- Hand sanitizer
- Eyeglass repair kit
- Spare glasses
- Small sewing kit
- Measuring tape

Protection

- Concealed (or open) carry firearm
- Extra mag
- Pepper spray or mace
- Whistle
- Don't forget your voice is a great protection as well

Unclassified

- Umbrella
- Two decks of cards

This concludes Section One: Everyday Carry! Great job. Now head over to Section Two: Vehicle Preparedness to tackle the next layer of preparedness—outfitting our vehicles. In Vehicle Preparedness, we're going to cover: what is vehicle preparedness, different levels of vehicle preparedness, seasonal vehicle preparedness, personalizing vehicle preparedness, and organizing vehicle preparedness. Now, turn that page and let's get to it.

SECTION TWO

THE PREPARED VEHICLE

> "Fascinations breed preparedness, and preparedness, survival."
>
> — Peter Benchley

In April 2011, something very unusual happened to our family. We had to spend a night away from our home without any notice. No going home to pick up a change of clothes, deodorant, shampoo, or even a toothbrush. No flossing our teeth that night. Imagine the morning breath we had the next day! That night we slept in our clothes and wore the same clothes and undergarments the next day. We didn't even have a comb or bush to untangle or smooth out our hair the following morning.

And we were not alone in this. "Since 2008, an average of 26.4 million people per year have been displaced from their homes by disasters brought on by natural hazards," a report from the Internal Displacement Monitoring Centre, an independent, non-governmental humanitarian organization studying displacement, reveals. "This is the equivalent to one person being displaced every second."[3]

One person *every second* is displaced from their home! That's staggering. And many of those people are not able to go back to their homes to get necessary items.

So what happened to us that night? My husband was preaching a Good Friday sermon in a small church in Bowling Green, Missouri. At the end of the service I got a call from my mother in a panic, wanting to make sure that we were okay. I assured her we were fine, informed her that we were in Bowling Green at a Good Friday service, and asked her why she was worried. She responded that our house was hit by a tornado.

The trip back to Ferguson from Bowling Green usually took an hour and a half. That night because of the condition of the roads and some being shut down, it took us almost four hours to get home. When we finally reached the intersection fifty feet from our house, police officers blocked off the road. We explained to them that we lived in that house. We showed them our driver's licenses with our address on them. It didn't matter. No one was allowed in the houses of the blocked area until daylight the next morning.

To make matters worse, my parents also lived in the cordoned-off area, which meant we couldn't spend the night with them. Fortunately for us, another family not too far from us opened their home for the evening. That didn't change the fact that we had no change of undergarments, toiletries, and none of our supplements or medicines.

Maybe you've looked back to see the name of this section again. "The Prepared Vehicle." At this point, you may be asking what "The Prepared Vehicle" has to do with tornados or other natural disasters. There's a very simple answer: If your vehicle is prepared with basic items and necessities, you will never find yourself without a toothbrush, change of undergarments, comb, or your medicines—ever again.

One of the principles we discussed in Chapter two – Creating Your Own EDC is that EDC functions in layers. The layers of EDC we discussed were what you keep in your pockets, what you carry in a small purse or bag, and what you carry in your backpack. I mentioned in that chapter that there is a fourth layer to your EDC: your vehicle kit.

In this section, we're going to cover topics like, what is a prepared vehicle? We're going to discuss various systems that we should have in place in our vehicle, and what each of those systems looks like.

We're going to tackle the topic of customizing our seasonal preparedness in our vehicle. Another big topic we're going to cover in this section is the personalization of our vehicle to care for our family. We'll also discuss how to practically fit everything into our vehicle, and how to organize and *find* all of our preparedness items.

CHAPTER ONE

DEFINING THE PREPARED VEHICLE AND DELINEATING ITS BENEFITS

> "There's no harm in hoping for the best as long as you're prepared for the worst."
>
> — Stephen King

We do a lot of traveling. Most of it is for my husband's work. Some of it is for my children to visit friends who live about six hours from us. We take a vacation once a year, and on occasion, we'll travel for me to speak. I don't know if this is true for you, but for us, "Murphy" likes to show up on trips. This year when we were on vacation, I got three spider bites and my entire arm swelled up. On other occasions, we've been driving on a three-hour trip and ended up with a flat tire. We've been stuck in traffic jams for— what feels like—hours. We've been eaten up by mosquitos at a wedding two hours from home. The list could go on and on.

When my arm swelled up, we had some homeopathic medicines on hand in our vehicle's first aid kit. When we got a flat tire, we had everything we needed to change it. When we're stuck in traffic jams, we had ways to entertain ourselves and our kids. Even when we're getting eaten up by mosquitos, we had bug repellent ready for the task. But if I didn't take the time to prepare my vehicle, do you have any idea how much money we would have had to spend? Preparing my vehicle for everyday—and even uncommon—emergencies saves us so much money, frustration, and headaches.

So, as we jump into this topic of vehicle preparedness, keep in mind the peace of mind you'll cultivate, the money you'll save, the headaches you won't get, and the anti-whine you'll be creating for your kids because you'll be ready for what life throws at you.

WHAT IS A PREPARED VEHICLE?

Before I jump into what a prepared vehicle is, maybe I should start with what a prepared vehicle *isn't*. A prepared vehicle isn't an armor-plated vehicle. It's not a Humvee stocked with three months' worth of supplies. We aren't pulling a storage trailer behind us so that we can carry even more, or if things get really rough, we could sleep several people in.

In simple terms, a prepared vehicle is an extension of my EDC. A prepared vehicle provides more complete coverage for my daily needs than my basic EDC in case of an interruption to my usual life and routine. It's a vehicle that's ready to handle any of life's minor emergencies (not the zombie apocalypse) while out and about or on a trip. Its level of preparedness is definitely beyond my EDC backpack, but it's not built to sustain my family and me indefinitely.

We currently have two vehicles. One is a full-sized van that mostly sits in our driveway unless we're taking a long trip. We discovered several years ago that a minivan didn't easily fit seven people and their luggage for a week or longer. Our other vehicle is a Honda CRV. This sees the majority of the action in our family.

Our vehicles look just like any other. Since I currently have four kids at home, the inside of each is cluttered just like yours. You won't see armored plating, a constantly attached trailer, or a big dog that comes with us for protection. We're not driving a "But-Out Vehicle," and I'm not suggesting you do either. We're taking the practical approach.

BENEFITS OF A PREPARED VEHICLE

I don't know about you, but I feel like there are times when I *live* out of my vehicle. A couple of years ago when I asked my husband a bunch of those funny questions in an "interview" that I got from Facebook, one of the questions was, "Where does your spouse spend most of his/her time?" His response, almost without delay, was, "In the car!" And he was right.

Even today, I took a vehicle out to go work on this book at a local coffee shop. From here, I'll be going to get a monthly medical treatment for a genetic condition, I'll go to a local restaurant to get a gift card for a new mama in our church, and I'll deliver it before heading home for a short time. After, I'll stop by a pharmacy to pick up a six-month supply of my only prescription med, then I'll pick up my oldest daughter for an hour and go to the same coffee shop from earlier. Then we'll head back home briefly for dinner, and after, I'll be in the car again to pick up my mom and father-in-law and take them and the kids to a piano recital. With the exception of maybe an hour for dinner, I'll have been on the go all day long. That isn't every day, but many days that's what my life looks like.

For me, asking if I should have a prepared vehicle is like asking if should I have a prepared home. I'm in it all the time! But not everyone is. For those of you who work outside your home, you'll likely have access to your vehicle whenever you need it. For those of you who don't work outside the home and are more homebody-oriented, are there any activities you leave your home for regularly? Maybe for church or visiting with a friend weekly? I used to go to a yarn shop and knit with others one night a week. Do you regularly use a gym?

Even with the work-from-home kick that many companies are on, I find that most people leave their homes on a fairly regular basis—even if it's just to pick up groceries they ordered from the grocery store.

You're ready for life's everyday emergencies

Let me give you just one example of how having not just a prepared but a well-organized vehicle has served our family well. We went to an outdoor wedding. It was a beautiful venue on a gorgeous day. But as soon as we took our seats, we started getting bitten by mosquitos. It wasn't just one and then fifteen minutes later another bite. It was multiple mosquitos at once, very often. Lucky for us, one of the things I keep in my vehicle is a homemade bug spray. I walked from my seat back to my vehicle and grabbed my bug spray. We didn't get bitten by any mosquitos the rest of the evening!

In another instance, we had taken a trip out to New Mexico. While we were at a rest stop on our way out, my kids were playing and one fell and scraped up their knees and elbows fairly badly. Because I keep a well-stocked first aid kit in my vehicle, I was able to take care of those scrapes without an issue.

I have a child who chronically suffered from motion sickness. We kept several things in our vehicle specifically for him including peppermints to calm an upset stomach—Don't believe that they work? You should try it! We also keep gallon-sized zippered baggies for when we didn't get peppermints to him quickly enough. And just in case there was a bit of a miss, we keep baby wipes in each of our vehicles.

Do you ever find yourself getting tired while you're driving? Did you know that having peppermints help with that too? If I get tired, I'll sometimes chew peppermint gum and that will, most times, perk me right up.

You save yourself time

Have you ever found yourself away from home with a headache? Most times, you can just "deal with it," right? But what if that headache starts getting pretty bad? Sometimes it's worth it to swing into a nearby gas station and buy one of those two-packs of Advil or Tylenol. But that takes time.

What if your child falls and scrapes their knee badly, but you're in a town that's over an hour from your house—do you swing by CVS or Walgreens and run inside to buy peroxide and Band-Aids?

Are you out running errands longer than you expected, and everyone is starting to get a little hangry? Running through that drive-through takes extra time. Drive there from where you are, sit in line to order, sit in line to pay, and get your food. Then pull over so you can get everyone's food distributed before you can drive off again.

You save yourself money

Each of the aforementioned scenarios also take money. I'm guessing you probably have Advil or Tylenol, Band-Aids, antiseptic wipes, and snacks at home. If you had some of each of those in your vehicle with you, you wouldn't have to purchase more of them while you're away from home.

But there are other ways having a prepared vehicle saves you money. If you notice your car is running just slightly warm and you know that you run through oil fairly quickly, you should check your oil level. And if your vehicle is low on oil, add some—carry an extra quart in your vehicle. But if you don't deal with the problem, you may end up burning your engine out and not even realizing it.

What if you're out and you get a flat tire, but your vehicle doesn't have a spare? If you have a can of Fix- A-Flat in your vehicle, you save yourself from driving on the rim of your tire which would likely damage it, or you save yourself a towing fee. Either way, you can save yourself a lot of money.

You save yourself stress

If I'm away from home and I encounter a problem because of a child or my vehicle or another person around me, and I have the resources to deal with it myself without taking much time, effort, or money, my stress level is *so much lower*.

I've taken my kids to the park before. You know how it is when you have multiple children of different ages. Child (age ten) is playing with his friend from church or school. Child (age six) falls and cuts him or herself. If you don't have any first aid supplies and have to leave, how does your ten-year-old react?

They probably get angry or at least upset because you *promised* them time with their friend. Of course, we explain that we need to take care of their sibling, but how much stress could be avoided simply by having items in your vehicle to deal with the problem then and there instead of having to leave?

You're ready for bigger emergencies in your vehicle

I'm guessing that most of us heard about the I-95 backup on January 5, 2022, that left hundreds of people stranded for up to twenty-four hours. This isn't something that happens every day, but being prepared to weather twenty-four hours on the road without home's creature comforts would have been invaluable to those stranded people. If they had had one or two liters of water per person to drink along with blankets, food, boredom busters (card games, books, audiobooks), and cell phone chargers, how many would have fared so much better?

You're (more) ready to leave at a moment's notice

A year and a half ago, both my husband and I got a notification on our phones that we needed to find shelter immediately, but be ready to leave our homes promptly when instructed. There had been a leak at a nearby anhydrous ammonia plant.

Because we knew that we already had toiletries, undergarments, food, and water in our vehicle, we didn't have to worry about grabbing those things. I do keep a list on hand of last-minute items to pack for our trips, which I did gather. And, yes, I had to go through our bug-out bags (personal emergency supply and food bags) to bring them up to date ('cause I didn't do it at the daylight savings time change—when conventional wisdom says to switch them out. Yes, I was delinquent). But having my vehicle well-stocked beforehand made our potential departure so much easier!

Recap and Looking Ahead

In this chapter, we have discussed the benefits of having a prepared vehicle – You're prepared for life's emergencies. You save yourself time and money. And you decrease your stress.

In the next chapter, we're going to dive into the nitty-gritty of how to prepare your vehicle. As you probably realized, there are different levels of vehicle preparedness. Being prepared for little emergencies around town is a whole different ball game than being prepared for a fourteen-hour-long drive through three or four states. So, join us in Vehicle Preparedness—chapter two. We're going to delve into how to get your vehicle prepared for around-town excursions.

CHAPTER TWO

BEING PREPARED FOR "AROUND-TOWN" EMERGENCIES

> "Better to have, and not need, than to need, and not have."
>
> — Robert A. Heinlein

Let's say you've been having a problem with your washing machine. You can afford to buy a brand new one, but trying to be fiscally responsible, you hire someone to come over and fix it for you. They arrive on the appointed day and time—which in the repair world is a miracle in itself. After they get in and you show them what your washing machine is or isn't doing—they nod and say, "Oh, I know exactly what's causing that. It's a simple fix and the part is easy to come by. But I left my tools back at the dispatch station, so I'm going to run back and get my tools. I'll be back in an hour."

How would you react? I know if it were me, my jaw would likely be hanging wide open. My instinct—not that I would follow through with it—would be to ask, "You're a repairman, right?"

"Oh yeah," the guy says. He points to the patch affixed to the front of his uniform. "I've worked for this company for five years."

"But you don't carry your tools with you?" I'd ask.

If his reply was, "Well, I wasn't sure I was going to need them," I would never hire from that company again.

Now that may seem like a silly scenario that would never happen, but does it? When you're out and about, do you ever find that you don't have the simple tools of your trade—whether that trade is worker, mom, entrepreneur, or grandma? Maybe it's just you, but whose responsibility is it to take care of you? Yours. So don't be caught without the tools of your trade.

LEVELS OF VEHICLE PREPAREDNESS

I break vehicle preparedness down into two levels. Level one: around town. These are the tools that you may need when you're not far from home. Level two: long trip. If you're on a long trip and you get stranded somewhere, you're going to need a different set of tools to get yourself home than you would if you were only a twenty-minute drive from home.

In this chapter, we're going to delve into Level One Vehicle Preparedness: around town.

VEHICLE PREPAREDNESS FOR AROUND TOWN

Not only does vehicle preparedness have levels, but like our EDC, we're going to break our preparedness into seven different categories or systems. Many of these systems will also translate into our homes when, in the next book, we start discussing home systems and how to prepare our homes for success, no matter what type of disaster we may face—man-made, economic, natural, or biological.

Our seven systems of vehicle preparedness include: Food and Drink, Sanitation, First Aid, Safety, Comfort, Shelter, and Vehicle Function and Maintenance. You'll notice that four of these systems overlap with our EDC.

What I want you to remember is that if you're new to setting up a prepared vehicle, I want you to get each of your vehicle's "in-town" systems up and running before you even begin to consider getting your vehicles ready for level two or your "long-trip" systems—especially if you aren't going to be much farther than an hour away from your home.

Food System

Level one of your food system is not having three whole days (or more) of food in your vehicle. Are you ever out and about near a mealtime, but don't want to run through the drive-through, and you're not *that* far from home? So, you tell yourself that you don't need a whole meal. Something as simple as a granola bar might do.

I keep various food items in small quantities in my vehicles. One box of individually packaged trail mix and one box of peanut butter crackers is all I need. I'm not feeding my family for a week, just for a snack. Since I have never, in my memory, needed snacks more than twice a week, I don't usually keep more than two snacks per person in my vehicle.

Since I grocery shop each Friday, if we've used up a set of snacks during the week, I simply replace them the next time I go to the grocery store.

Most vehicles have consoles between the front two seats—this is a great place to keep snacks.

What types of snacks store well in a vehicle?

There are so many different kinds of snacks. I recommend walking the snack food aisle of your local grocery store to find items to stash in your vehicle. I'll offer some ideas, though.

For my children without food allergies, we love peanut butter crackers, cheese crackers, fruit snacks (which are allergen-free), pretzel packs, and cookie packs.

For my husband and I—who prefer to eat low carb, we can keep meat sticks (like Slim Jims), Whisps (real cheese baked to be like a cracker), single servings of almonds, cashews, or peanuts, packets of tuna fish, BBQ chicken, salmon (with a spoon), or freeze-dried strawberries or blueberries.

For my kids who have gluten intolerances, we keep trail mix single-serve packets, gluten-free cracker packets, granola bars, fruit snacks, Fruit Roll-Ups, and "Crunchy Rice Rollers." One of our favorite brands of gluten-free bars is Enjoy Life. They have bars that even our picky kids enjoy. Our gluten-free children can also have all the same snacks that my husband and I eat.

Drinks

Now, drinks are admittedly a little more complicated. I know that regular single-use water bottles, the kind that you buy in a 40-pack from Costco, can leach BPA and antimony into the water. The consistent ingestion of these can lead to cancer and other diseases. But the key word for me is consistent. If we keep a small case of these in our vehicle, and we dip into these once a year, I'm not concerned about getting cancer from drinking out of these. I'll level with you: we keep a case of water bottles in our vehicle.

If you don't want to go this route, there are several ways to handle this. I know several families that have purchased stainless-steel water bottles for each member of their family, and they don't leave the house without their bottles. It's a bit more money up front, but it works. That way everyone always has something to drink.

A similar option is Hasle Outfitters' four- or eight-pack of 17 oz. food-grade stainless steel water bottles. Google this and you'll find it's a great way to go for keeping your water free from contaminants and rust. You could fill these three-fourths full of water and keep them in your vehicle year-round. You may want to keep them in an appropriately sized cooler for two reasons. First, by keeping them in a cooler you're providing an extra layer of insulation, even though these water bottles are insulated. Second, you're keeping them contained. They can't roll all over the place in a cooler. During the winter, if you keep them wrapped in a blanket inside the cooler, it will help insulate them even more, but how well will depend on where you live and the temperatures your area gets down to. That is why I suggest only filling them three-fourths full if you plan on leaving them outside in freezing weather.

Something else I've done—and I have researched this—is to keep drink boxes in my car. I haven't found any evidence (actual or anecdotal), statistics, warnings, or anything else that says not to keep these in a vehicle. I keep drink boxes in my vehicle. I'm talking about tetra-packed juice boxes. I know that they can safely be frozen, so there's no danger in the winter. In the summer, I'd probably change these out at least once a month, but they would provide your family with something to drink in a pinch without going to a drive-through.

Additional items relating to food

In case this is the first book of mine you've read, I want to tell you that I am a *very down-to-earth mom*. I don't live in the world of zombie apocalypses—though preparedness is very important to me. Because I'm just a "normal" soccer-type mom (minus the soccer), I keep regular items that relate to food in our vehicle. I keep a picnic table cover along with picnic table clamps. I also keep trash bags, zippered bags, wet wipes, and/or baby wipes in our vehicle. There are times when we want to picnic and we don't want to haul a whole bunch of equipment out, so it makes sense to keep it in the vehicle—and each of those items can have multiple uses if we ever did (God forbid) get stranded.

Around-Town Sanitation System

When we talk about sanitation in our homes, normally we think of keeping things clean, having running water, and working plumbing. While having a decently clean car may somewhat parallel sanitation in a house, the rest of the concept flies out the window!

Here's a scenario. Have you ever been driving down the road while eating a burger or other sandwich, wrap, or burrito (uh-huh, I know you've done that part, don't deny it), and a blot of ketchup smears across your face as you take a bite of the juicy (but completely bad for you) burger? Well, the answer to that lies in sanitation!

How about this one? You're driving along and all of a sudden from the back seat come the infamous words, "Mom, my stomach is upset." That statement is immediately followed by an oh-so-unpleasant sound. Uh-huh, sanitation!

Or it's that time of the year and your allergies are acting up. You sneeze, followed by a second sneeze, followed by about ten more. You look around in desperation for a tissue, a napkin, or anything (other than your clothes) to take care of your dripping nose. Sanitation to the rescue!

Let's tackle issues of sanitation in your vehicle.

Upset Stomachs

When I was pregnant, I was the culprit. Today, it's usually one of my kids. I'm sure it's not just my family where upset stomachs and moving vehicles go hand-in-hand. Having two things in place will prevent future problems and fix current problems that can sneak up on you.

We have seatback organizers in our car. In the seatback organizer behind the driver's seat, we keep zippered bags. I keep gallon-size and quart-size bags in one of the pockets. Whenever someone has an upset stomach, we grab one of the baggies so they have it when they need it. If their stomach does indeed decide to empty its contents, you or your child has a place do to so.

In another of the pockets, we keep a container of baby wipes. They're cheaper than Wet Ones. If one of our children does happen to empty the contents of their stomach, but they make a little bit of a mess in the process, we have baby wipes to clean them up. Another option would be to keep a towel in the back of the vehicle in case of an emergency, and this would definitely qualify!

As for prevention of the aforementioned calamity, we also keep a stash of peppermints. The flavor of peppermint almost always quiets an upset stomach. I don't always keep these in the seatback organizer though, because if I did, they wouldn't last. With four kids getting in and out of our CRV almost every day, they would disappear quickly! I keep these stashed in the back of the CRV, so they're less likely to get into them.

Trash Trouble

Finding a way to take care of trash in your vehicle is an important part of sanitation. If you're tripping over old water bottles or slipping on granola bar wrappers (granola bars sound so much healthier than candy bar wrappers, huh?), having a place to put your trash is rather important.

We keep a car-specific trash can in our van. It keeps things clean and uncluttered. We also keep trash bags, both larger black ones and smaller white ones, just in case. Trips may require a bigger trash receptacle, but this works for now.

If You're of the Female Persuasion

I'm sure many of us ladies have regular cycles. Even if you're as regular as clockwork, now and again you might get a surprise. Having feminine hygiene items in a vehicle comes in handy! Make sure you include these somewhere. I keep these in a backpack that stays in the back of my CRV.

Stuck Away From Home?

During the Good Friday debacle that I mentioned earlier, a friend offered to let the six of us—including one very pregnant mama (due in only about three months) stay on several couches in their living room. That was amazingly kind of them, but we did have a problem. As I mentioned earlier, we had nothing with us. By the next morning, we were truly a sight.

Since then, we've adopted two things that have made a huge difference if we ever get stuck away from home. In a backpack that stays in our vehicle, we have one quart-sized zippered bag with one change of undergarments for each person. The phrase "never again" is so apropos here!

Besides one pair of unmentionables for each family member, we also have a baggie of toiletries. In this baggie, we keep: shampoo, deodorant, lotion, toothpaste, toothbrush, powder, cotton swabs, floss, soap, a comb, ponytail holders and clips for us girls, two different kinds of shoelaces, a washcloth wrapped around an old pair of glasses (for those of us who wear and still have an old pair of glasses) in case ours get broken, a pair of fingernail clippers, a mini flashlight, and a P51 can opener.

If we had these items when we were unable to return home one evening, it would have made our lives so much more comfortable. This all falls under the heading of sanitation.

Sanitation encompasses so much, from baby wipes to toilet paper, zippered bags to trash receptacles, and "unmentionables" to feminine supplies. I can't tell you how many times I've been thankful to have these items on hand!

AROUND-TOWN FIRST AID

You're out at a park with your kids, and they're having a blast. For summer, it's a fairly cool day in the mid-80s. The sky is the soft blue of a lovely day. Even with the blue of the sky, there are plenty of clouds to douse the intensity of the sun from time to time. There are your kids again. Their squeals of delight pull your attention back to their smiling faces. Dontcha just love hearing them laugh raucously as they slide down the twisty slide or play hide and seek in and around the playground? It's almost bliss. Then, *it* happens. You've just looked from one child to another, and you hear that blood-curdling, "I just got hurt" scream. Are you ready? There are three types of parents. There are parents who practically wrap their children in bubble wrap and never let them have any real fun. Don't be that parent.

There are parents who let their children loose in the world. When something happens to that child, there is nary a Band-Aid to be found, let alone anything to clean the wound with. And what's Neosporin?

Then there's the prepared parent. They quickly assess the situation. No bones sticking through the skin. Okay, that's a good thing. No deep gashes spurting blood. Check. Superficial scrape, but bleeding quite freely. What do you do and what do you have in your arsenal?

I probably have all my bases covered in my EDC backpack. But what if the scrape needs more than a regular-sized adhesive bandage?

Enter the car kit. In this kit, we keep Dental Medic, ammonia inhalants, nitrile gloves, paper and pen, super glue, tons of different types and sizes of adhesive bandages, gauze sleeve, rolled gauze, first-aid tape, self-adhesive ace wrap, a finger splint, Tylenol, low-dose aspirin, alcohol wipes, tweezers, a container of Q-tips, cotton balls, and gauze pads.

We've only had to dive into this a couple of times, but it's been helpful to have on each occasion we needed it.

Preventative First Aid Items

We also keep items in our vehicle which aren't meant to help heal us but to prevent us from getting ill. We've already mentioned peppermints to prevent stomach upset and to help keep people awake. But we also keep sunblock, bug spray, lotions, and an umbrella. While the umbrella seems stupid to put on the list, it is super handy! My skin is fair. I burn easily. Having an umbrella around on sunny days allows me to use it as a parasol to keep the sun off most of my body so I don't get burned. Besides that, when I'm exposed to the sun for longer periods, I also get migraines. Using an umbrella as a parasol helps that too. It also helps keep me or other people dry so that there's less of a chance we'll catch a cold because we're cold and wet.

CAR PROBLEMS/CAR SYSTEM MAINTENANCE

It's happened to us all. Actually, it's happened to my family way too much! We find ourselves in these crazy circumstances when it comes to our vehicles. About two years ago, we were on our way back from a Wednesday night Bible study. Because my husband worked late, he met us there, so we had two cars. We were driving back from Bible study after dark. My husband was about four minutes ahead of us in his car. We always took a highway home from the study, and this week was no different. We pulled onto the ramp and headed down to merge onto what looked like a very clear road. But it was dark, and I didn't see a full-sized tire rim in the road as we started to merge.

We ran over the thing and I heard a kerplunk followed by a series of cyclical thuds. We had a flat tire, and as I thought at the time—*Who knows what else!* But it gets even better. As we tried to make our way over to the right shoulder of the road, we weren't the only ones who ran over the tire—four other vehicles ran over the same stinking tire! And one of them. . . yep, you guessed it, was my husband.

While I only had one flat tire, he had two and only one spare. No, it's not a regular thing to get two flat tires at once, it was something we couldn't have foreseen.

What Items Should We Carry that Deal With Maintaining Our Vehicles?

The Owner's Manual. So often, vehicle problems that we stress over—like, *What does that light mean?*—are simply solved by looking it up in your owner's manual.

Jumper Cables. We've all done it from time to time. You turn the car off and accidentally leave the lights on. Maybe you turned an overhead light on in your vehicle and forgot to turn it off, or maybe your battery or alternator is just about to go. Whatever the reason, having jumper cables are a must. But I'm going to one-up this. Recently, I was introduced to a device called a Halo Bolt. This little—and by "little" I mean about 10"x5"x2"—device will jump your car for you! It even comes with a mini set of jumper cables. Besides jumping your car, it will also pump up your car's tires! It can charge a cell phone, or you can use it to charge your computer. It's a very handy little gizmo.

A Spare Tire, Jack, and Tire Iron. These usually come with the vehicle. Start simply by checking to make sure that your vehicles all have their own spare, jack, and tire iron to change your tires.

Basic Tools. Did I mention that I'm not mechanically inclined? I mean, not at all. That doesn't mean that I don't need a toolkit. Whether it be my husband, my roadside assistance person, or a person willing to help a girl out, having these on hand will help others help me.

Windshield Washer Fluid. This is especially helpful in winter when the slush gets kicked up onto your windshield by the car in front of you. Running out of windshield washer fluid is scary at best, and dangerous at worst. I buy a small bottle. It's easier to keep than a full-sized bottle. This stays stashed in the back of my vehicle.

Tire Gauge. Does one of your tires look low, but you aren't quite sure? If you have a tire gauge on hand, you can find out for certain. And it's foolproof. Even I can work one of these puppies.

Tire Sealant, Aka Fix-A-Flat. This is a lifesaver! If you have a tire that has an annoying slow leak, keeping this on hand can save the day!

Ice Scraper. 'Nuff said.

CARING FOR COMFORT AROUND TOWN

In reality, when we're close to home, if we have food for our bellies and water to quench our thirst, there are very few other items that we truly need for our comfort. If it's warm and our AC goes out, we can put our windows down. If it's cold and our heater goes out,you bundle up with a blanket that you've stashed. I don't care how close you are to home, when it gets below zero in our neck of the woods, cold is the word of the day.

For our "Around-Town" Comfort System, we travel with seven easily mushable—yep, I just coined a word—fleece blankets. I purchased them from IKEA a couple of winters ago. They are cheap, work really well, and are excellently "mushable."

Another option for keeping your family warm during winter—when you have to be out of the car and standing in the elements for a while—are hand and foot warmers. We carry these in the back of our CRV. I try to keep fourteen pairs of each since there are seven of us, and we may need to use them more than once before replenishing.

PERSONAL SAFETY AROUND TOWN

A different way of looking at safety for your vehicle is, "What items do I need to be safe in my vehicle?"

I think there are a bunch of great answers including a car "Safety Hammer Emergency Escape Tool." This tool allows you to both cut your seatbelt and break the glass of a window in your vehicle. It's an important tool to keep you safe while you're in your car.

Another item that you should consider is a fire extinguisher. Amazon has a great one that is rated for car usage. It's small (compared to home fire extinguishers) and can safely be left in your vehicle whether it's very cold or very hot.

Another item to consider is a pair of work gloves. We used to get the one-dollar gloves from Harbor Freight, but guess what? They're one-dollar-quality gloves. As of this writing, Costco has a three-pack of really nice leather work gloves for around twenty dollars. That's almost a steal.

If you get stranded at night, you'll find that having a headlamp is wonderful for several reasons. The biggest is that you don't need to hold a flashlight while you're changing a flat tire or looking under the hood to see why your car is overheating. It also makes you much more visible while you're moving about beside the road.

Along those same lines, having glow sticks are wonderful if you have children. These work for making kids visible if they're out of a vehicle and walking alongside a road with you. They are also fun toys for kids. I've never seen a kid who doesn't enjoy a glow stick.

Reflective triangles or flares can also be a blessing. They help get people's attention so that just maybe they get over into the far lane instead of blowing past you in the near one. It may also incline a good Samaritan to stop and help.

Recap and Looking Ahead

In this chapter, we've covered six systems we can put into place in our vehicle to take care of everyday, around-town emergencies. We talked about how to have food and drink items on hand for when we need a pick-me-up and out running errands. We talked about sanitation and how to be prepared for sanitation emergencies when you're close to home. Whether at the park, the library, or the grocery store, we've discussed what we need to be ready for first aid emergencies. We also worked through items that we can keep on hand for effectively handling car maintenance and minor repair issues. We covered how to provide our family with things to keep them comfortable while we're in our vehicle. We ended the chapter by discussing personal safety and what that looks like when we are in our vehicles.

But in the next chapter, we're going down the rabbit hole deeper still. We're going to talk about each of these topics for when we're out of town or traveling somewhere. We'll be adding another system to the six we've already mentioned: shelter. What do we need to consider when we're taking a trip more than two hours from home, and how does our preparedness in our vehicle change in light of that? Turn that page, and let's delve into Vehicle Preparedness for the long haul.

Action Items:

1.) Grab a piece of paper. Fold in it half long ways and short ways, creating eight equal rectangles front and back. Label each section with one of the following: Food and Drink, Sanitation, First Aid, Vehicle Mechanics and Maintenance, Protection, Comfort, and Shelter.
2.) In each section, start jotting down ideas for things you'd like to add to your vehicle for each system.
3.) Go through your list. Gather the items you already have and put a checkmark by them on your list.
4.) Prioritize the items you don't yet have and start picking them up as you have the means in order of priority.

CHAPTER THREE

VEHICLE PREPAREDNESS FOR THE LONG HAUL

> "Spectacular achievement is always preceded by unspectacular preparation."
>
> — Robert Schuller

I've read my share of prepper fiction where someone gets stranded away from home during a crisis of some sort—usually an EMP (Electromagnetic Pulse)—which disables all electronic equipment. In a previous chapter, I've already mentioned the first book in A. American's *The Survivalist Series*. My favorite EMP book is *One Second After*. It's about a small town in the mountains of North Carolina when an EMP hits. Makala Turner, one of the main characters, just happened to be driving through Black Mountain when any item that has any electronic components goes kaput. She has nothing but what is with her in her car. In both books, survival is based on what is in their vehicles with them or the kindness of strangers.

Our family takes at least three long trips a year. By long, I mean that we drive at least six hours away from home. Two of those trips are usually a fourteen-or-*more*-hour drive from home. The thought of getting stranded away from home hit me hard. I must admit, often when I take a long trip, I feel the need to make extra sure that I have enough of the right tools with me to be as prepared as I can be if something like this happens while I'm on the road. It was in systematically thinking through these scenarios that I developed these long-haul vehicle preparedness systems we're going to explore.

No matter which system we're discussing, to decide on my long-haul items I ask myself, "If I were stranded, what items would I need to carry with me to take care of my family if we had to stay where we were stranded?"

Before we jump into talking about each system, I want to remind you that you should make sure that your "around-the-town" systems are in place first. That doesn't mean you shouldn't read this chapter. Just file the information away for a few weeks as you finish getting your "in-town" systems ready to go.

VEHICLE FOOD SYSTEMS FOR THE LONG HAUL

When I asked myself that question in relation to food and drink, I started brainstorming through what items I would want or need to care for my family. There were several: (1) A way to cook food (2) Something in which to cook food or boil water (3) Items on which or with which to eat the food. (4) Water filter(s) (5) Water storage containers.

I didn't include more food in that list, and we'll discuss that a little later.

Let's start with a way to cook food. I needed a stove of some sort. I looked at a bunch of different types of stoves. I wanted one that allowed me to use anything as a fuel source, nothing that required the purchase of single-use disks. The stove that I landed on is called "Ohuhu Backpacking Stove." What drew me to it were these words taken directly from the Amazon page: "What's Great About This Stove is Its Wide Compatibility with All Sorts of Fuel Types. Not Only Can You Use a Traditional Gas Tank Or, Solid Fuel Tablets, but You Can Also Use Any Type of Wood You Might Bring or Find Along the Way."[4] I don't have to store fuel tablets, but I can if I want to. You can use those Sterno stove cans or chafing dish cans with this as well, but I wouldn't store those in my vehicle.

Besides having something to cook *on*, I wanted something to cook *in*. After much looking, the most compact and best-quality set I've found is called, "MalloMe Camping Cookware Set." We have used this and it's a little on the smaller side, but let's be honest, I wanted compact, and compact it is! In a box that measures approximately 6.5" x 6.5" x 4", I got ten items including a 4 ½-inch-tall pot with a lid, an almost 2-inch-tall frying pan, two bowls, a cleaning loofah, wooden spatula, soup spoon, spork, and a carrying bag. It is made of aluminum which I prefer to avoid, but if I'm using this to cook, it's either the end of the world or as close as I will probably get. I won't be worrying about aluminum at that point.

So, I found something to cook on and something to cook in, and now I wanted something to eat from. This was easy. There are so many wonderful, heat-resistant collapsible products now, it was almost a no- brainer. I purchased a silicon collapsible bowl and a spork/knife set for each family member.

Foods for the Long Haul

What about food? I said earlier that I don't keep food in my vehicle long-term. This is why. When we go on a long trip, we always bring our snacks, and for a family of seven, it's a lot. Also on long trips, I pack our seventy-two-hour food tote. I'm not afraid I'll get stranded close to home and not be able to get home. I'm really only concerned when I'll be driving more than an hour from home, so I'll add items like the seventy-two-hour food kit. Yes, it's only three days, but that does buy us three days to figure things out without adding a whole refrigerator of food to my vehicle.

Let's talk about what I keep in my seventy-two-hour food tote.

We want things that are (1) as compact as possible (2) as lightweight as possible (3) don't require much preparation—except perhaps heating water.

I've handled meals this way.

Breakfast is two packets of oatmeal per person per day and either an instant coffee packet (don't forget non-dairy creamers and sweeteners if you need those for your coffee) or a packet of hot chocolate mix.

Lunch is one of two options: either crackers, peanut butter, and jelly, or mylar-packaged meat (tuna fish- flavored or otherwise, salmon or BBQ chicken, and crackers. Each person will get one of those, a granola bar, and a single-serve drink mix to dress up their water. The containers of peanut butter and jelly are from Amazon. The crackers are in a box that we can make last for three days. Another option here—if space were less of an issue—is one or two single servings of just-add-hot-water mac and cheese cups.

You can even get these gluten-free.

I get creative with dinner. Have you seen those bags of "just add water" soups? I get the Bear Creek brand from my local grocery store. But you can find so many different types just by searching online. I obviously don't have a pot big enough to cook the whole thing, so I plan to have everyone get out their bowls, and I will divide the mix evenly, and heat the water for one to two people at a time. You can keep an extra box of crackers for dinner or a trail mix packet or granola bar. It's not a ton of food, but it will keep you going.

Dealing with Water for the Long Haul

In Chapter two – Being Prepared for "Around Town" Emergencies, we talked about stainless steel water bottles for your vehicle. If you went ahead and purchased them or added them to your priority list, you're already a step ahead! Everyone will have something from which to drink. Now you need to make sure that everyone has safe water.

So, let's talk about having, finding, or purifying water. We've opted for two different water filters and two different water containers. We have long kept Berkey water bottles in our vehicle. What I like about these is that you can carry water in the bottle and it filters as you drink it. With a product like a Lifestraw, you can only use it at the water source itself, meaning you can't carry any of it with you.

That's why we prefer a Berkey water bottle. The other type of water filter that we've invested in is a Survivor Filter Pro. It will filter 100,000L of water before the filters need to be changed! You can also purchase filter replacements to extend the life of your Surivor Filter Pro as many times as you have filters. Something else that we like about this filter is that it pumps water from a water source and filters it, but you do need to have a second container for your water.

The only downside to using a water filter like this is if you want to take water with you away from the water source, you'll need containers. Well, if everyone has a water bottle, that's one great way to do it. Another thing we have are two one-liter stainless steel canteens. We also carry with us two two-liter leakproof water bladders which fit inside a backpack. This gives us a total carrying capacity of more than eight and a half liters of water when we take into account six of the seventeen-ounce stainless steel water bottles. That will cover a family for a couple of days if stretched carefully.

VEHICLE SANITATION FOR THE LONG HAUL

Remembering that the long-haul portion of any system is for trips that are going to be more than an hour or two from home, sanitation systems for this level are much less complex than the additions I suggested for level two of the Food System.

I don't know about your family, but in ours, the need for the body to empty itself of the beverages and food it has consumed is the most common sanitation need we experience on long trips.

Gotta Go?

When we take a long trip, we stop at least once *every two hours*. Even with these regular stops, now and again we'll be traveling down a remote strip of road and we'll hear from the back, "Mom, I need to use the restroom *now*." I don't know why their bladder didn't alert them fifteen minutes ago or why it wasn't articulated to us if it did.

What do you do if you're out in the boonies and there's no restroom for miles around but the urge strikes? Well, if you're a guy (even my littlest guy), most times it's not that big of a problem. Find a tree.

But for us ladies, it can be a bigger issue. Without going into detail, there's a device that will allow a woman to pee standing up. It's called "Go Girl." You should check it out.

What if nature strikes from the other end? You need to have two things on hand. Remember those zippered bags I talked about? Yeah, those. You know what to do with them. You'll also want to have toilet paper somewhere handy or use the baby wipes I've mentioned. Please never leave fecal matter anywhere. Animals can, and probably will, eat it, and it will make them sick. If you prefer toilet paper to baby wipes, mush the roll as flat as you can and take the cardboard tube out. Most regular-sized rolls of TP will then fit into a quart-sized zippered bag.

But what if you've run out of zippered bags? This is where carrying a small folding shovel in your vehicle will come in handy. You will need to dig a hole more than six inches deep, do your business, and cover the hole again when you're done. If you run out of TP, make sure you grab some leaves to clean yourself off when you're done. They can be buried with the rest of your business. Just be careful of poison ivy.

Another item that you may want to consider for sanitation and long trips is a solar shower. I know a regular shower wouldn't be important, but there will be times when you need to clean your body of grossness and goop. Besides, a solar shower is small, lightweight, and easily stashed in your vehicle kit.

FIRST AID FOR THE LONG HAUL

For long trips, we've put together a much more comprehensive first aid kit. Because we travel all over the United States on the eastern side of the Rockies, we need to be prepared for a bunch of different situations. Our kit is a large craft kit that I purchased from Michael's using a 40%-off coupon. This particular box looks almost like a toolbox on top with three drawers below. Michael's no longer carries this, but I looked up "toolbox with drawers" on Amazon and found almost an identical one (heavy-duty plastic with three or four drawers) for half of what I paid at Michael's. You may want to look into something like that.

Because of the size and bulk, we only take this with us on long trips. Under the lid, I keep my big items: peroxide, alcohol, iodine, "Be-Cool" forehead cooling bandages, an Israeli style tourniquet, Dental Medic, medic scissors, a sting and bite extractor kit (snake venom), hand lotion, lip balm, and an eyeglass cleaning cloth.

If you open the front, you'll find three separate drawers with lids. In our first drawer, we keep hydrocortisone cream, nystatin, triamcinolone ointment, Benadryl spray, Neo To Go spray, a thermometer, thermometer sheaths, lighted tweezers, fingernail clippers, Monistat cream, and two eye droppers.

The second drawer contains Bayer aspirin in case someone is having a heart attack. We also have Pepto tablets, acetaminophen, Excedrin, New Skin, nasal spray, Blink eye drops, Equate pain reliever, Prid drawing salve, and alcohol wipes.

The bottom drawer contains sterile 2x2 gauze pads, corn pads, all sizes of Band-Aids from very large rectangles to the smallest "dot," circular non-sterile gauze pads, wound seal, wound seal for nosebleeds, first-aid tape, and self-adhesive wrap.

Almost everything from the EDC and the car kit is duplicated here; we didn't want to have to remember what bags contained which items if there was a true and larger emergency. It just made sense to have a larger kit that had pretty much everything.

CAR MECHANICS/MAINTENANCE ISSUES FOR THE LONG HAUL

In Chapter Two - Being Prepared for "Around-Town" Emergencies, we delved into car maintenance issues. Most times, I've found what you need for around-town maintenance issues is very similar to what you need for longer trips.

I do want to offer a couple additional suggestions for when you're planning a long trip.

The first thing you should consider before taking a long trip is getting your car looked over by a mechanic. We routinely do this about twice a year anyway. We'll take our vehicle in for a level three oil change. Besides the oil change, they run the entire vehicle through a rigorous inspection. I don't want to get halfway on a business trip to North Carolina and get stranded because I didn't realize one of my tires was almost threadbare and have it blow on the interstate. I'll know if I have any mechanical issues, or will shortly—whether those are brakes, shocks, or belts that need to be replaced or changed. This way I also know all of my fluids are full.

But let's say I did that inspection two months ago and we're getting ready to take our annual trip to Florida. Well, there are still a couple of things I'll do. I pick up an extra two quarts of oil. One of our vehicles goes through about a quart of oil every three thousand miles.

So we need to make sure we've checked our oil before we leave, and I'll take one or two quarts with us just in case.

If you're traveling during winter, having an extra half-gallon of windshield washer fluid would also be wise.

PROVIDING COMFORT FOR THE LONG HAUL

Before I dive into what to add for a long-haul comfort system, I want to discuss two types of comfort. Being prepared is more than just having some extra paper towels, bowls, and food stashed in your vehicle. Being prepared also means being ready for two of the biggest problems you face as a mom, especially when kids are trapped in a moving vehicle. "Mom, are we there yet?" and "I'm bored!" Those two are one of the everyday types of emergencies we'll face a million times more when stranded in the middle of nowhere without food, water, and internet. Being able to comfort and care for a child no matter their age is helpful, especially when you're trying to deal with other issues.

Then there's a second type of comfort. It's cold out and the heater broke on your vehicle yesterday and your appointment to get it fixed isn't for another two days. This is taking care of the physical aspects of comfort that crop up in our vehicles from time to time. Let's take a look at each of these in turn.

Emotional Comfort and Fun

Do emotional comfort and fun go hand in hand? If one of my children in particular thinks the fun factor is low, his emotional comfort level is commensurately low. How do you help provide emotional comfort and fun in your vehicle? Here are a couple of things that we keep in our vehicle for such instances.

Keep a rousing book on hand in your vehicle. Is there a book that you know your kids would love, but you've never read it to them? Keep a copy of it in your vehicle. If you're traveling and your CD player, DVD player, or Bluetooth connection breaks on you, you have a way to keep the kids occupied as long as you have one other reader in the car with you. A similar option is to keep several audiobooks downloaded on your phone. You could play one of those if things get dicey on a trip or even when you're stopped at a hotel.

Whether your family likes to play Spades, Crazy Eights, Uno, or Skipbo, keep cards in your vehicle. Playing cards will help your family occupy their time if something happens to derail a trip. I keep two decks of playing cards in my vehicle. But I don't just keep the cards. I keep the book *Hoyle's Rules of Games* in the car too, so that we can always learn a new game or refresh our memory on the rules of a game we haven't played in a while.

A few years ago, I made five two-week-long trips to Kansas City to have IV chelation once a day during that period. Each time I went I would bring my kids back a small gift so I could show them in a tangible way that I missed them. So, I would head over to Five Below to look for gifts. While I was there, I discovered several different varieties of travel-sized board games: Monopoly, Connect 4, Trouble, and Clue! The games are about 6"x9"x2". The box folds out to form the table on which the board rests so it can be played even if you don't have a table. Making it easy to play them in a car, alongside a road, or in a hotel room.

On a different note, still dealing with comfort, if you have a younger child, having a spare stuffed animal or "lovie" is really important. When my (now sixteen-year-old daughter) was two, we headed on a trip to Pella, Iowa, and were there for a good part of a week. While we were there, we lost the stuffed polar bear she carried with her everywhere. Do you think we could console the child? No. There was no consoling her, and I couldn't find a replacement bear anywhere.

Do yourself a favor and buy a duplicate stuffed animal for your little one. If one is lost or you left it at home, you can still help your child feel the comfort that they get from their special stuffed friend.

So, now that we've discussed ways to help our family feel emotional comfort, let's talk about preparedness that deals with physical comfort.

Physical Comfort

There are several ways to help those in your car cool down if it's hot and your AC seems to be working improperly. The first, obvious answer is to put the windows down and forget about your hair. But if for some reason you aren't moving and everyone is hot, there are these nifty things called cooling towels. My personal favorite is called "Frogg Toggs," a cooling cloth. You wet it and its surface temperature drops 30 degrees! These also absorb a lot of sweat, and in doing so it moistens the towel which in turn keeps the temperature of the towel low and keeps you cool. There are ones that you can wear around your neck and others that are meant to drape over your face. There are smaller ones that are 3"x29", whereas the larger towels measure 33"x19."

But let's say that instead of it being hot out, you're stranded and it's cold. Keeping your body warm is important. Having those mushable fleece blankets that I talked about in the last chapter is great, but there is another option. You can keep your body much warmer by using Mylar blankets. However, Mylar blankets only reflect the heat that your body gives off. What if they aren't enough? You can keep your body even warmer by layering your mushable blanket with a Mylar blanket over it. I mentioned Mylar has wonderful reflective properties, so your body's heat will gather in the mushable blanket and reflect toward your body. A similar option is something called a Tac Bivvy. These are reusable (though not highly sturdy) Mylar sleeping bags.

PERSONAL SAFETY FOR THE LONG HAUL

There are just three extra items that I would add for personal safety.

The first is a phone charger. Making sure you can keep your phone charged on a long trip is a safety issue. This could be having a cigarette-lighter-compatible charger in your car. This could be having a portable battery pack. Don't forget the cords that you might need to go along with these. Another possible option is a solar-power phone charger. If it's a sunny day, you could put the solar cell on the dashboard and hook your phone up to it.

The second important item I believe you need for any trip longer than a day away is a phone mount for somewhere in your vehicle. I've had several different kinds where you set your phone's pop socket into a compatible car mount. If you don't have dash space, like us, a vent-mounted phone holder is a great option.

Now obviously, as I drive down the road I'm not going to be watching a movie on my phone, but on long trips, I almost always use Google Maps, and having the information and route displayed on my phone where I can easily see it makes everything so much safer for my entire family.

What if, however, you *thought* you were charging your phone, but it wasn't plugged in all the way, and your phone battery completely dies? There's one more item I highly recommend for your vehicle's Level Two Safety System, and that's a paper map.

My family and I were traveling home from Ohio to Central Illinois. We stopped in Indianapolis to eat dinner with some friends. My phone was fine when we went into the restaurant for dinner and dead when we got done. My husband didn't yet have a smartphone—this was about ten years ago. We literally didn't know which direction we needed to go to get home because we were sitting at an odd junction of several highways, and we had to go on one to get to the other. Get a map or nationwide driver's atlas. When you have a paper map, you can find where you are and navigate an area whether on foot or the road.

SHELTER SYSTEM

In 2013, the James Glanton family (two adults and four children ages two to ten) decided to take a trip to Northern Nevada which ended in a way no one imagined. The family of six skidded on icy roads and their car went over an embankment and flipped over. Being fifteen miles from the nearest town, with sub-zero temperatures, they decided to stay put. They had food and water in their vehicle. James burned the jeep's tires for warmth and used the fire to heat rocks to help keep them warm as well. They were rescued two days later. When you hop in your vehicle, you never imagine that you're going to have to shelter there, but there are circumstances in which you may be forced to.

Ways to Extend the Shelter Capacity of Your Vehicle

How can we plan for shelter and keep items for shelter in our vehicles? Tarps are truly multi-purpose items. You can use a tarp as a covering for a shelter or you can use it to block at least some of the light from a fire from a road if you don't want to be seen. Tarps can be used as ground covers if everything is damp and several people need a place to sit. If you opt to keep tarps in your vehicles, make sure to also carry cordage.

Another shelter option would be something simple and lightweight like two-person tents. You can find these as cheap as $30 on Amazon and some even have four-star reviews. Most of them are lightweight and very easy to set up and take down. If you were stranded during a crazy and unlikely situation like an EMP and needed to get home, a short two-hour drive would take you around twenty-five hours of walking to get there. You'd probably have to divide this up into two to three days of walking time and need a shelter of some sort. It's not fun or glamorous to think about, but be practical as you prepare your vehicle even for mid-range trips.

Pieces of Wisdom for Using Your Vehicle for a Shelter

There are two pieces of general wisdom to be shared when dealing with a vehicle as a shelter system. First, when you're leaving your home for a while or going more than an hour away, you need to let someone know where you're going, the route you plan on taking to get there, when you plan on arriving, and that you'll check in with them when you arrive.

This way if something happens to you when you're on a trip, someone knows where you were headed and what route you were planning to use. If you don't make it back or don't contact the person expecting you, your contact will be able to send someone out to search for you sooner than they otherwise would. And if you gave them your route, they'll know where to start the search.

The second is that you should *never* leave your vehicle unless it isn't safe for you to remain. Your vehicle is much easier to spot than you will be if you aren't in it. Before you consider leaving your vehicle, you need to ask yourself if there's a good reason why you shouldn't stay here. If your vehicle fell into a stream, then absolutely get out. If your vehicle slid into a precarious spot from which it could fall farther, absolutely get out. But if there's no reason not to stay, you should stay in your vehicle.

Recap and Looking Ahead

As we close out this chapter on Vehicle Preparedness, remember that this is meant for long trips, as our needs are much greater if we're stuck away from home for longer periods of time. It's easier when you break it down into each system: Food, Sanitation, First Aid, Comfort, Car Maintenance, Shelter, and Personal Safety.

But we're not done with Vehicle Preparedness just yet. Join us in the next chapter as we delve into the issues that surround Vehicle Preparedness during different seasons, what you need to consider for summers and winters, what should be changed out, potential problems you might encounter, and how to better be ready to tackle each of them. Flip the page, and let's jump into seasonal Vehicle Preparedness

Action Items:

1.) On the worksheet you started for Vehicle Preparedness, chapter two, in each rectangle, draw a line under where you finished your in-town part of each vehicle system.
2.) Under the line, using this chapter and brainstorming your ideas, add what you'd like to carry with you for long-haul trips.
3.) Go through what you already have in your house and garage—keeping size and weight in mind—and put a checkmark by the items you already have.
4.) Create a priority list of the rest of your items. Please keep in mind, you should have your short- term items in hand before you start focusing on long-haul items.

CHAPTER FOUR

SEASONAL VEHICLE PREPAREDNESS

> "Preparedness when properly pursued is a way of life not a sudden, spectacular program."
>
> — Spencer Kimball

Monday, January 3, 2022, started as a normal day. People got up, got ready for work, and hopped on the interstate to get there. Some were still on an extended holiday from school or work, so many decided to head out to do something fun. In areas that didn't usually see snow, like Virginia, snow was falling. Of course, that meant a lot of kids wanted to be out in it.

The problem was that the snow kept coming in Virginia. Now I used to live in Virginia. I'm not exaggerating when I say, upon moving there (after having lived in Erie, Pennsylvania for sixteen years) we would wake up on any given morning and hear, "We're expecting an inch of snow today. . . and now for the school closings." Virginians didn't know how to drive in the snow—and before we moved, we lived in snow-central and were very used to getting a foot of snow at a time.

So here, these unsuspecting people in Virginia had a hard time driving in the snow. During this unexpected snowstorm, a traffic jam shut down an entire fifty-mile section of I-95 amidst the foot of snow. In January. . . in the snow, people were stranded for over twenty-four hours. Many vehicles ran out of gas, meaning there was no heat for their vehicles either. It's the ultimate nightmare for a parent. And it sounds strangely post-apocalyptic for our day and age.

What these Virginians needed in their vehicles on that day was vastly different from what they needed 95% or more of the year. It was winter, and many were unprepared. In this chapter, we're going to discuss seasonal vehicle preparedness. What do you need specifically for summer or winter? How do you adapt what you've purchased to be ready for the different challenges that the extreme seasons pose? That's what we're going to cover in this chapter. Let's jump in.

SUMMER

What makes summer vehicle preparedness different than vehicle preparedness in general? Two of the things that we love about summertime are sunshine and fresh air! The problem is that there are consequences that come along with wonderful sunshine and fresh air. So, from spring through fall, we need to make sure we have sunscreen in the CRV. We've discovered that spray sunscreen (as opposed to the kind you squeeze out of the tube or bottle) tends to discolor your clothes. If it's just you, you can find sunscreen in travel sizes. If you have a family, get a big one. There are plenty out there! You could even make sunscreen by doing an online search for "Sunscreen Recipes."

Another thing you need to make sure you keep in your vehicle during the spring through fall is bug spray. There are so many different diseases you can get from mosquitos, even here in the main body of the US where it's not swampy. Keeping the buzzing critters away is more than convenient—it will help keep you safe. You never know when you're going to need bug spray.

Summertime also means hot temperatures in your car. A 2002 San Jose University study found that, "Temperatures in enclosed cars with a basic gray interior rise approximately 19 degrees F in 10 minutes' time; 29 degrees in 20 minutes' time; 34 degrees in half an hour; 43 degrees in 1 hour; and 50-55 degrees over a period of 2-4 hours."[5]

Especially when you have little ones that are susceptible to heat, having something in your car that can help block out the heat is important. Even if it's just you or you and a spouse, hot cars are just uncomfortable! One way to keep the heat away is by using a sun visor—a great summertime addition to the car. They can be found at auto parts stores, Walmart, or other box stores.

Another spring-through-fall consideration is being prepared for an unexpected deluge if you get stuck in the middle of nowhere. I don't want to carry seven mini umbrellas or four really big umbrellas in my vehicle. I think if we're honest, we know that umbrellas only keep your top half dry for a while, but not your bottom half. Rain ponchos may be a much better prospect because wearing one keeps your hands free and tend to keep more of your body dry. Ponchos are small and flat when they're folded up and can be tucked into small spaces. It's a great option.

Summer fun!

Depending on where you live, summer can bring other activities. One of the things that we like to do during the summer is go on picnics. I don't care that my kids are now eleven through twenty years old— they still love to pack up a few sandwiches and chips and head to a park.

So there are a few extra things that we keep in our vehicles specifically for the summer. We have two picnic table clothes and eight picnic tablecloth clamps. We also like to keep at least two lightweight blankets in the CRV even in the summer, so we can drape them over a picnic bench if it's dirty. That way we don't soil our clothes during the picnic—well, unless we spill food on them. But did you know baby wipes get most stains out of clothes if you catch them early enough?

Time at the Seashore

Do you live near a beach of some kind? Are you there often? There may be a few things you want to keep in your vehicle. Flip-flops are a great (and relatively space-saving) alternative to wearing your regular shoes onto the beach and getting your car filled with sand.

Carry a beach ball with you. It's inflatable—meaning it takes up very little space. Remember those two blankets I mentioned above? They're great to sit on at the beach as well.

Do you like to go to the beach at night? There are inflatable solar lanterns called Luci Lights. Another option would be solar-powered yard lights. These work really well in the sand at the beach. Each of these would make a great summer addition to your vehicle!

Food and Drink in Summer

Interestingly, food and drink pose challenges both in summer and in the winter, but for different reasons.

In the summer, you may want to be cautious of regular water bottles because the constant heating of the water will leach chemicals out of the plastic, depositing them into the water within the bottle. I briefly mentioned this in Chapter two – Being Prepared for "Around-Town" Emergencies. Again, stainless steel water bottles are a great option.

We also should talk about food. Earlier in this chapter, I quoted from a study saying that in two to four hours of your car being in direct sunlight, the interior can heat up fifty-five degrees! So if your vehicle was at seventy degrees in the summer, it could get to 120 degrees within two hours. In "A Year Without the Grocery Store," chapter three, I talk about the five enemies of food storage. One of those enemies is temperature. Here's what I say there:

> "The warmer the air temperature where you store your food, the shorter the time it will remain edible. Certain prepackaged food storage meals will keep for five years if you keep them at a steady fifty degrees. If you store those same prepackaged foods at sixty degrees, they are good for up to four years. If you store them at eighty degrees they are good up to three years, but if you stored them at 120 degrees. . . they would only be good for one month."

Hmm, "but if you stored them at 120 degrees. . . they would only be good one month." And we said that in two hours our cars can get to what? Oh, lookee there, 120 degrees. So, you need to be careful of the food that you choose to store in your vehicle and make sure you're swapping it out regularly.

Summer is one extreme. We have another one that I like a lot less. Let's delve into discussing the cold season, its pitfalls, and how to overcome them.

WINTER

When winter rears its ugly head, it brings a different set of challenges. In winter, we need to deal with cold, traction problems, and freezing temperatures. So, let's talk about what we can do to prepare our vehicles for winter.

Vision Issues

One of the things I detest about winter is having to scrape ice off my vehicle. On the farm where we currently live, we don't have a garage. We have a Morton building, but it's not the same. While we are considering reorganizing the building for this winter to park there, it wouldn't matter. If you live in an area where you ever get any snow or ice, please get a car scraper. Invest in a good one. You don't want it to break halfway through the winter.

And as mentioned previously, don't forget windshield washer fluid.

Slippery Conditions

Winter—at least in my neck of the woods—means slippery conditions. Fortunately, we live on a well-traveled road, which means it's cleared and salted regularly, but not every road we drive on is. There are different ways to keep your vehicle safe on the road. Let's discuss some of them.

Did you know that by adding extra weight to the back of your vehicle, you can help your car stay safely on the road? Don't just put bags of potting soil or something like that in the back of your vehicle to weigh it down. Take something useful. Sand and kitty litter are both heavy because they're dense. You might be thinking, "Karen, I don't have a cat. Why in the world would I want to carry kitty litter in the back of my vehicle?"

I'm so glad you asked. Kitty litter isn't just good for controlling litter box odors. It has a very practical use around the house, which we'll discuss in the next book in the series—so keep your eyes open for that. It also helps with traction.

What if that extra weight from the kitty litter doesn't keep you on the road? If you slide off the road and get stuck in a ditch or get caught in a flat but muddy area, you'll need something to help you gain traction. Putting kitty litter in front of and behind the tires that are stuck in the mud, snow, or ice can help create an area of traction for your wheels. This will help you get out of the mess.

Kitty litter isn't the only thing that will work in this scenario. Sand can also help you if you get stuck. You can also wedge cardboard under your tires to help you gain traction. Cardboard is lightweight, and folded flat it doesn't take up a lot of room. It's just that one piece won't add any weight to the back of your vehicle to help keep you on the road.

If you live in an area that gets truly treacherous weather, you may be familiar with chains for your tires. When I was growing up in Erie, PA, it really didn't matter what the weather was like. We never stayed in because of snow—unless we literally couldn't get to the end of the driveway. One of the ways that my father dealt with the conditions was to put chains on our tires. This gave us extra traction and safety in difficult driving conditions.

Food and Drink in Winter

Do you keep water in your car? As we've already discussed, winter can cause problems. Plastic water bottles—even if (for reasons that I delineated in Chapter two - Being Prepared for "Around-Town" Emergencies, you kept them in your car from spring through fall—cannot be stored in your vehicle in the winter. The freezing isn't the issue. Most of us know that when water freezes it expands; if you leave plastic water bottles in your vehicle in the winter and your area freezes, you'll end up with partially filled water bottles and a wet trunk.

I know we talked about this earlier in the book: using stainless steel water bottles is an option, but make sure you don't fill those full either—even if they are vacuum-insulated. There's no guarantee that the water won't freeze, and you'll lose the bottle that you paid so much for—besides having a wet trunk.

And how much do you keep back there that could be ruined? Another option would be to keep your water bottles in an insulated cooler with a blanket wrapped around them. That will help keep your water bottles from freezing.

What about food? Most foods will not be ruined by freezing, however, the constant freezing-and- thawing cycle can be an issue. Do you keep meat packets in your vehicle? You know those packets of tuna fish in Mylar that you can tear open and eat? What about the barbeque chicken? Or pulled pork? You don't freeze meat, thaw, and freeze it again. It isn't a good idea to keep these in your vehicle in the winter.

So if you shouldn't keep those in your vehicle, what should you keep—especially if you're diabetic and you need low-carb snacks? We keep cured meat sticks and beef jerky in our vehicles even during the winter. There are some delicious low-carb bars that should be fine in the winter, although if they freeze, they'll be harder to eat. Some nuts are another great low-carb option. Whisps should also be fine for those who need low-carb.

For everyone else, options abound. Trail mix is still good in the winter, just be careful when you try to eat the candy-covered (M&M-like) chocolates, as they might be hard on your teeth. Crackers should be fine. Single-serving sizes of chips should be fine. Just be careful with anything that is normally in a semi- liquid state or something that will get really hard when it freezes.

Staying Warm

Okay, we saved the most obvious issue for last.

I have a friend who works as an assistant to a midwife in Illinois. Two years ago, during a snowstorm, she was stuck for twelve hours on the road on the way to a birth, but this mama of four (at the time) was ready. Let's talk about some of the things she did right.

Before she left, she was well bundled up. She had on a nice warm coat, gloves, and a hat. Her footwear was appropriate, and she was wearing warm socks. Maybe it should go without saying, but anytime you (or your stubborn kids) go out in the winter, make sure you're appropriately dressed!

When she left, she had a hot drink in an insulated mug. This helped her insides stay warm for a while. She also had blankets in her vehicle. She was able to wrap up in the blankets to keep herself warm. Hand and foot warmers were also a winter staple in her vehicle. She was able to use those to keep her extremities from getting frost-bitten.

Other things you can carry with you include Mylar blankets, which we've already mentioned. These are single-use, but fold down into 2"x3" and they're less than ½" deep, but some open out to measure 4'3"x6'9". That's not a bad size when expanded. Just make sure that you check the size of your Mylar blankets when you purchase them.

Recap and Looking Ahead

In this chapter, we covered summer and winter seasonal vehicle preparedness. Each season offers different challenges. For summer, we have to overcome sun, bugs, and temperatures, while still being ready for fun activities. In the winter, we have to deal with visibility, slippery roads, food and water issues, and staying warm in cold temperatures.

In the next chapter, we're going to discuss how to organize our vehicle preparedness. How do we make the most of our space? How do we fit the most items into the space we have? How do we find what we need to find quickly? How do we maintain our organization and keep our items up to date? How do we keep ourselves from running out of items or make sure that we replace items we run out of?

Action Items:

1.) Start with a piece of paper. On the front, write "Summer." On the back write, "Winter."
2.) On the front of the paper, using your area of the country and its normal weather conditions, make a list of items you need to store for summer. If you live near the coast and go to the beach a lot, make sure to list out the items you'd want with you for an impromptu visit to the beach. If you go hiking in the summer and there are things specifically needed for your hikes, make sure you include those.
3.) On the back of the paper, using your area of the country and its normal weather conditions, make a list of the items you need to store for the winter. Do you go sledding often? What do you want to make sure that you always have with you if friends invite you to go sledding or snowboarding, etc.?
4.) On your phone's calendar program, set reminders for checking through your items and swapping them out for the changing of seasons.

CHAPTER FIVE

VEHICLE ORGANIZATION

> "Remember: When disaster strikes, the time to prepare has past."
>
> —Steven Cyros

Having items in your vehicle is incredibly important. Just as important as having items in your vehicle is putting them into your vehicle in a way that: makes sense; keeps them together in predefined places; ensures you know where they are; and allows you to get to them when needed. In some ways, it's a much more daunting task. Unfortunately, those areas are usually an afterthought, but those are what make your preparedness effective.

Now, there's an elephant in the room. If you did the action items from chapters two, three, and four of this section, you might have started laughing at me, saying, "Karen, I have a (fill-in-the-blank small car), there's no way I'm going to fit all of that in and still go to the grocery store."

To illustrate my thinking on the matter, I'll tell you a story.

Have you ever seen or heard about the presentation where a professor stands in front of his class, and he has a quart-sized glass jar? He holds it up for his students to see. "See this jar?"

They respond aloud or nod their heads.

He takes about seven or eight decent-sized rocks, and one at a time carefully drops them into the jar. "Is the jar full?" he asks, showing them that he can't fit the next rock of the same size into the jar.

His students say, "Yeah, it's full."

Out from under his podium, he pulls out a jar with medium-sized pebbles. Again, he carefully and slowly pours the pebbles into the jar and shakes the jar several times in the process. Eventually, he gets as many pebbles as he can into the jar. He raises his eyebrows and asks his students, "Is the jar full?"

Well, the last time they said yes, and it wasn't, but they can't see how he could fit more in. Some say it is and some say it's not. Nodding his head, he sets the jar of pebbles aside and pulls out a jar of pea gravel. Repeating the process, slow and steady, he taps the jar against his podium several times to help everything settle. A smile and a quizzical look creeps across his face. "Is the jar full?"

This time only a couple of his students say, "Yes." The rest, starting to catch on, say, "No! Fill it fuller!"

And as if by their command, he sets the pea gravel aside and pulls out some fine sand. Laughter is heard throughout the room. Taking his time, he pours the sand in, tapping the jar up and down, pouring more, and tapping again. When it looks like there's no way that he could get even another grain of sand into the jar, he turns to his students and holds the jar up with a big smile on his face. "It is full?" he asks.

This time there's a resounding, "No! Fill it fuller!"

He nods with a delighted grin on his face and sets the sand off to the side. This time from beneath his podium he pulls out a small pitcher of water and holds it up for everyone to see. His class breaks out into laughter and cheers. He pours the water into the jar until it's up to the top of the jar.

Then, turning to his class one last time, he holds up the jar and says, "Now, the jar is full."

Your vehicle is like that jar. You start by putting the big stuff in. It's so easy to believe that it's full, but you still have so much space. In this chapter, I'm going to show you how to fill your jar. I'm going to help you find those previously unthought-of spaces and create space. I'll help you organize things so well that you can fit more than you thought possible into the space that you have.

As a matter of full disclosure, I've owned everything from our five-passenger CRV to a fifteen-passenger "behemoth," as I refer to it. I will grant you that on long trips, we take the fifteen-passenger van (with a third of the seats removed because we need the space). That being said, when we go on vacation, we usually have eight people in our vehicle. So it's fair that we need a larger vehicle, but for shorter trips up to eight hours long, when we only have three of the kids with us, we travel in our five-passenger CRV with all our luggage and all of our preparedness equipment. So, I understand "small."

MAKING THE MOST OF LIMITED SPACE

When you think about putting things into your vehicle, I can guarantee most of you think first about the space in the trunk. While you'd be right—there is more usable space in the trunk than in the front. But there's so much more space in your vehicle than the trunk. Let's look at those areas.

The Front of the Vehicle

Most vehicles have similar storage spots in them. In the front of the vehicle, most have a glove box. Many have a console between the seats. Every vehicle that I've been in in the past five years has storage space in the doors. That's just the front!

Glove Box

Ask yourself, what items in your vehicle do you use the most? Do you use sunglasses while driving or riding in your vehicle? Maybe you should keep them there. In my opinion, every front seat should have a seatbelt cutter/glass breaker within reaching distance. Do you use napkins or tissues a lot? They may fit in the glove box as well.

I can see you all nodding. I can also see some of you saying, "But Karen, that would be a jumbled mess if I just tossed those in there." And if you just tossed those in there, you would be right. Did you know that there are glove box organizers that are made to fit different models and years of cars? Humor me and (even if you refuse to buy anything from there) go search Amazon for "Glove Box Organizer Toyota 4Runner." Go ahead. I'll wait for you.

Okay, did you find a nifty plastic thing that organizes your glove box into different-sized spaces? Yep, I'm betting you did. So if you, like me, want your car to be visually appealing as well as organized, then there's a tool for that.

Let's say that you don't find a glove box organizer to fit your specific space because maybe you have an older model. Well, there are other options. When I searched for glove box organizers, I found these nifty little organizers that look like zippered planners. If you open it up, there are spaces for your vehicle's instruction manual and other car-related items including a place for a tire gauge. You could use two or three of those to organize your space. Just make sure to label them.

How else could you use that space? If your first aid kit came in a zippered bag or you could place it in one, that might be the perfect place for it.

Center Console

I know that not every car has a center console. I know this because our Ford Transit doesn't have one, but if it's "car-like" as opposed to "van-like," most often there is a console. This is prime real estate. In most of our vehicles, this is where I keep our snacks. If I have a good divider, I'll also keep napkins in it. Depending on the size of your console, you can use this space for other things. Maybe you keep a contained survival kit alongside your first aid kit.

I don't know how you want to organize your car, but make sure you don't just use this space as a catch- all or for trash. Give it a name and a purpose.

Door slots

Most doors have slots in them to store items. If you organize any of your car systems into little bags, this might be a great place for them. If the bag is full, or you have three or four in each slot, it likely won't fall out or slide around.

Space between the seat and the console

Did you know there are companies that make devices that fit in that narrow gap between your seat and the console? Yep! There are. So, what can you put in those? How about a pad of paper and several writing utensils? In the other, perhaps tissues or napkins? Again, name and use this space.

The Back Seat of the Vehicle

Okay, so we've talked about the small underutilized spaces in the front of your vehicle. Let's talk about more of these in the back seat.

Space Behind the Front Seats

One of my favorite ways to create space in the back of the van is to use two seatback organizers.

For the last ten years, our main vehicle has been a minivan or a full-sized van. I feel like I had almost limitless storage space. Oh, was that ever nice. My minivans had decent storage space most of the time. But about halfway through 2021, we decided to do something absolutely crazy and downsize one of our vehicles. As you've already read, we chose a Honda CRV as our second vehicle. There is decent legroom in the back seat, though not a ton.

That said, it doesn't have the storage space of our full-sized van or even the depth of storage space of our previous minivans. So how do I fit everything into our CRV? I have several organizational items that I use to great effect. We have two seatback organizers, one for the back of each of the front seats. In these we keep our zippered baggies, a package of baby wipes, large and small trash bags, homemade bug spray, glow sticks, a small notebook called a "fat book" (Google it. I love them!), a pen, clicker pencil, sharpie, car-specific fire extinguisher, four stainless steel water bottles, several travel-sized packages of tissues, and at least one smaller umbrella. Right there, I've more than doubled the space in the back seat.

Don't forget the space behind those! Behind your seatback organizers, often vehicles have their own handy-dandy pouch! Make use of this. We oftentimes put our large country-wide map book in this slot. It's also a great place to stash some coloring books and colored pencils if you have kids. Use the space for a couple of books or card games. Again—name and utilize the space.

Under the Front Seats

Now, this won't work in every vehicle, but in some vehicles, you can fit things under the front seats— from the back seat. If your vehicle has this capability, look for flat things that you can put there. This might be a great place to use one of those zippered organizers that's only about 1" – 1 ½" tall, but 8" long and 6" wide.

Back of the Vehicle

What makes dealing with the back of the vehicle more of a challenge is that there is open space, but we need to find a way to contain what we place here. There are two ways to go about this.

First, you can use one container with different parts. The biggest tip I can offer is to get a trunk organizer. The one that I have is by TrunkCratePro (yes, all one word). Their motto is, "There's no junk in this trunk." Dontcha just love it? Ours is the large and measures 24"x14"x12.5". If that's too big for your family's needs, there are smaller sizes. There's even an extra-large one which measures approximately 36"x 18"x12.5". We use this in our van when we're going on trips.

What's even better than it fitting well in a trunk is that it's modular. What I mean is that it comes with Velcro dividers that can be organized in a bunch of different ways. We divided ours in half and stacked some of our bigger items on one side. On the other side, we subdivided it into two smaller sections.

There are also pockets on the outside. When our van was our primary vehicle, in our TrunkCratePro, we kept space blankets, a first aid kit, a "MalloMe" camping cooking set, a portable outdoor camp stove, work gloves, cordage, an extra knife, matches, a 9-volt battery and steel wool (you can start a fire with those two), two water bladders, a Survival Pro Water Filter, two one-liter canteens, travel silverware, collapsible bowls, a tarp, bungee cords, and feminine supplies.

In the separate outside pockets, we've kept picnic table clamps, fire starters in another, decks of cards, the Hoyle card game book, and a large flashlight. It's wonderful. You're going to find that so many of (if not all of) your preparedness supplies will fit in this! Use it. We still keep ours in the van, but as I've said, I now drive the CRV.

The thing is, even with all those items in there, it doesn't look cluttered.

ORGANIZATION

Let's talk about effective ways to organize your items. There are three different approaches, which are: grouping like items together; by usage; or a combination of the two.

Like Items Together

This is the method that would easily describe the trunk of our CRV. What I love most about it is that there's a removable shelf which practically doubles our storage space for the back. We keep the top of the shelf clear except for our reusable grocery bags for Aldi runs. However, under that shelf is where we keep our vehicle preparedness items.

Think back to our Vehicle Preparedness systems—how many did we have if you don't include shelter? Six. I have space for six small totes. Now, it's not a true one-to-one, one-tote-for-one system, but it's close. I use one tote for first aid, one for sanitation, one for vehicle mechanics/maintenance, one for comfort and safety, but two for food and drink. My canteens, water filter, stove, cooking pots, and dishes all take up a lot of space. So, they get two totes.

What's even better is beside the six totes, I also fit my tent, backpack (with prepper supplies), a case of water, a large roll of paper towels, and an empty second backpack (in case we need to leave the vehicle and want a backpack to carry items with us). All that fits under the shelf as well.

By Usage

For you, organizing by usage may make the most sense. In this system, the items you use most are closest to where you sit. Do you get into your snacks often? They should be close. Tissues? Yep, keep them close. Do you use your map often? How about baby wipes? Plastic bags? The more you use an item the closer it should be to you.

There are also things you will rarely use. These can go in the trunk—perhaps in a trunk organizer. Maybe you've never used playing cards on a trip, and though you see the value in it, you don't feel like you need it near you—it goes in the back. Fire-starting supplies? Yep, in the trunk.

A Combination of the Two

We employ a combination of these two methods in our family. I want to have our snacks close at hand. We need to have zippered baggies nearby. Napkins and tissues both need to be easily accessed. A few peppermints need to be hidden, but easily grabbed. Wet wipes? We use them often. These are the types of things we keep in the front and back seats of our CRV, but as I previously described, we keep our preparedness supplies in the back organized by system.

Find What Works for Your Family and Your Vehicle

When we get a new vehicle, I always end up taking some time to look it over and ask myself where are its nooks and crannies that I can exploit? What do I need in this vehicle that I may not have needed in other vehicles? How do I plan to organize my items?

As you start working on your organization, you shouldn't just ask yourself questions about your vehicle, you should ask yourself questions about your family. Are there only three of you? Maybe you only need one seatback organizer and a small trunk organizer. Are there ten of you? Well, you might need two trunk organizers, three or four seatback organizers, and two backpacks. Remember, one size never really fits all. Customize—even your storage—for your family.

Finding What You Need Quickly

We were out hiking one day, and one of my children fell and scraped their leg. I brushed the dirt off as best as I could without anything with me for this short hike. When we got back to the van, I went in search of our first aid kit. I couldn't find it. I mean, there are only so many hiding places in a van, right? I stashed it so well, I couldn't find it.

Because of that debacle, I came up with a system. On my phone, which is pretty much always with me, I have an app called Cozi. It's a family calendar and list app. On that, I created three lists.

(1) Front of the car
This contains subsections of glove compartments, console, doors, and between the seats.

(2) Middle of the car
This contains subsections of under the front seats, behind the front seats, hidden compartments, and seatback organizers.

(3) Trunk
This contains subsections of trunk organizer, backpack, backseat organizer, and misc. trunk space.

Now, I never have to wonder where anything is. If I need to find my first aid kit, all I have to do is to open that app and flip through the lists.

Recap and Looking Ahead

In this chapter, we've covered a lot of ground. We've talked about the different nooks and crannies you can find to utilize space in your vehicle. I've shown you ways to layer space (putting seatback organizers in front of car pockets) and reminded you to use them both. We've talked about different organizational methods for making sure you get the most out of your trunk space.

But we're not done, quite yet! In the next section, you're going to find a very useful appendix. While I always want you to personalize your items for your family, I will lay out suggestions for items that you may want to consider keeping in your vehicle for both Around-Town and Long-Haul Vehicle Preparedness.

Action Items:

1.) Take an honest look at your vehicle. Where do you have space you can utilize? Where have you not utilized your space?
2.) As you begin to assemble the tools for your various vehicle systems, start to group things together in like locations. Find the right container to keep things in.
3.) As you begin to fill your vehicle with the items you're gathering, make sure to notate where each item is in electronic form. Organize this by the front of the car, middle row of the car (if you have a middle row), back seat of the car, and trunk of the car.
4.) If you need to, further subdivide the space on your list, i.e. "seatback organizer 1, seatback organizer 2, under driver's seat, under passenger's seat," etc.

ADDENDUM

VEHICLE PREPAREDNESS CHECKLIST

> "Circumstances can force your hand. So think ahead!"
>
> — Robert A. Heinlein

Now—and only now that you've walked through how to choose things for your vehicle list—just like I did for your EDC, I want to take you through my Vehicle Preparedness lists. Not because I want you to copy my list—please, please don't. I want to encourage you to think through things, and maybe my list will help you think of something you might have missed otherwise.

Food and Water

Short-term

- Snacks
- Stainless steel water bottles or plastic water bottles
- Drink mix packets

Long-haul

- Stove—we use an Ohuhu Backpacking Stove
- Water filter (Survivor Filter Pro, Berkey Water bottle, and/or LifeStraw)
- Cooking kit—we use MalloMe
- Water bladder
- Stainless steel canteen
- Collapsible bowl and silverware set per person
- 72-hour food tote

Sanitation

Short-term

- Tide pen
- Peppermints
- Car-specific trash can
- Feminine products
- One pair of undergarments per person
- Quart-sized zippered baggie per person each with
- Shampoo
- Deodorant
- Lotion
- Toothpaste
- New toothbrush
- Travel powder
- Cotton swabs
- Floss
- Soap
- Comb
- Ponytail holders and hair clips
- Shoelaces
- Washcloth wrapped around an old pair of glasses
- Fingernail clippers
- Mini flashlight

- P51 can opener
- Baby wipes
- Gallon-sized zippered baggies
- Quart-sized zippered baggies
- Black trash bags
- White trash bags

Long-haul

- GoGirl
- Survival shovel
- Toilet paper (tube removed and transported in a quart-size zippered bag)
- Solar shower

First Aid

Short-term

- Dental Medic
- Ammonia inhalants
- Nitrile gloves
- Paper and pen
- Super glue
- Adhesive bandages
- Gauze sleeve
- Rolled gauze
- First-Aid tape
- Self-adhesive ace wrap
- Finger splint
- Tylenol
- Low dose aspirin
- Alcohol wipes
- Tweezers
- Q-tips
- Cotton balls
- Gauze pads

Preventative First Aid

- Sunblock
- Bug spray
- Umbrella
- Lotion

Long-haul

- Peroxide
- Alcohol
- Iodine
- "Bee-cool" forehead cooling bandages
- Israeli-style tourniquet
- Dental Medic
- Medic scissors

- Sting and bite extractor
- Hydrocortisone cream
- Nystatin
- Triamcinolone ointment
- Benadryl spray
- Neo To Go spray
- Thermometer
- Thermometer sheaths
- Lighted tweezers
- Fingernail clippers
- Monistat cream
- Eye droppers
- Bayer aspirin
- Pepto Tablets
- Acetaminophen
- Excedrin
- New Skin
- Nasal Spray
- Blink eye drops
- Equate pain reliever
- Prid drawing salve
- Alcohol wipes
- 2x2 gauze pads
- Corn pads
- All sizes of Band-Aids
- Circular non-sterile gauze pads
- Wound seal
- Wound Stop for nosebleeds
- First-Aid tape
- Self-adhesive wrap

Vehicle Mechanics/Maintenance

Short-term

- Owner's manual
- Jumper cables
- Spare tire
- Car jack
- Tire iron
- Basic tools
- Windshield washer fluid
- Tire gauge
- Tire sealant
- Halo-Bolt Air

Long-haul

- Trip to the mechanic to check systems
- Extra quart or two of oil
- Windshield washer fluid

Winter-Specific Items

- Ice scraper
- Kitty litter or sand or cardboard
- Snow chains

Comfort

Short-term

- Fleece blankets
- Picnic table cover
- Picnic table clips
- Hand warmers
- Foot warmers
- Mylar blankets
- Cooling blanket, i.e. Frogg Togg
- Card games
- Book(s)

Long-haul

- Hoyle's card game rules book
- Specific card games—Uno, Skipbo, Phase Ten
- Travel games—Connect Four, Trouble, Clue

Safety

Short-term

- Safety hammer emergency escape tool
- Fire extinguisher
- Work gloves
- Headlamp
- Glow sticks

Long-haul

- Phone charger
- Cord for charger
- Car mount for phone
- Fire starters
- Dry bags

Shelter

Long-haul

- Tent
- Tarp
- Cordage

We have one chapter left. Make sure to flip the page and head to the conclusion where we'll tie it all together!

CONCLUSION

> "Preparedness is the ultimate confidence builder."
>
> — Vince Lombardi

What would being prepared mean to you? How would you feel if you were really prepared when you left your home today? If you knew that you had everything you needed on your person, close by, easily accessible, or in your vehicle, would it change the way you interact with the world? What would it do for your peace of mind? What would it do for your confidence level? What would it do to your sense of satisfaction?

I'd love for you to take a minute and think about the next time you plan on leaving the house. Maybe you plan on leaving tomorrow morning to run some errands or to go to work. I want you, mentally, to watch yourself getting your stuff together before leaving. What do you grab? Think through the contents of the items you grab as you head out the door. Then picture yourself arriving at your destination, but as you get out of the car, your foot slips and you scrape your elbow up badly. It's not deep, but it's bleeding freely. Are you ready for that with what you grabbed on your way out of the house? Do you grab an errant half-used napkin from your car and decide to go back home because you aren't able to take care of the situation? Or do you grab a clean napkin because you know where they are and they're well-stocked? You keep pressure on the spot while you grab your first aid kit. You clean it off with an alcohol wipe or peroxide. You dry it off, spray some Neo To Go, and have the right Band-Aid. Because it's an elbow, you wrap some self-adhesive bandage around it. After that, you clean up your mess and go about your business. You don't need to go home because you were prepared. Because of that, you've saved money—in gas for an extra trip home. And you've saved time, because you'd still need to run your errand later.

Now I want you to picture yourself again. This time you're running late to an appointment, but because of a last-minute phone call, while you were getting ready to leave you weren't able to get lunch. You're in your car driving, but you don't have any time to stop between where you are and your appointment.

Can you take care of your hunger? And if you can, what will that do for the quality of your appointment? If you're walking into a business meeting, will you feel better able to tackle things head-on if you don't feel hangry? If you're teaching a private lesson, will you feel more calm and confident if you've had a chance to put something in your stomach? Or even if your appointment is for something like a pedicure, will you be more patient as the tech works on your feet if you've been able to eat a snack or two that were in your vehicle?

Again, I want you to see yourself on vacation with your family. GPS has rerouted you onto a back road because there's a traffic jam on the main highway. Your five-year-old says, "Mom, I need to go to the bathroom." There's no gas station for miles, and you check your GPS for a nearby restaurant. There's nothing.

You nod and say, "Okay. Give me a minute and we'll see if we can find a tree." But instead, your son says, "No, I need to poop, Mom." How do you handle it? Are you ready with what's in your vehicle? If you're ready, you know you have everything you need to handle the situation no matter how inconvenient. You know you won't leave waste behind that can harm an animal. Your child doesn't have the embarrassment of defecating in his pants. You've saved yourself the time of having to clean up a child and digging through suitcases to find clean clothes. You've saved your family from the stench of a mess in the vehicle. You've made your entire—albeit undesirable—situation so much better because you were ready.

My desire is for you to be ready. I would love to know that you're ready for every one of these scenarios and more. Why? Because you're better than everyone else? No. Because you know more than everyone else? Nope. Not that, either. It's because I want you to be confident, bold, and at peace no matter what life throws at you.

If, as you worked through the book, you decided to take the time to go through each Action Item, in the end you likely realized the decisions you made and the actions you took will, in part, determine your future success when you are on the go.

You've got this, Mama!

WHAT'S NEXT?

> "Failing to prepare is preparing to fail."
>
> — John Wooden

Congratulations are in order! You've finished the book and worked through the action items setting you well on your way to being prepared when you're out and about with your family.

But where do you go from here? Well, this is just one book in the series! The *Are You Prepared, Mama?* series currently has four books written or planned. You've just completed *Mom on the Run*, and as moms, aren't we on the go? The second book is already underway - ***Mama's Home! Preparing Our***

Home for Life's Emergencies. Books three and four will be announced as I move along through the process.

IN THESE UNCERTAIN TIMES,
YOUR FAMILY CAN GO
a year without the grocery store!

A YEAR WITHOUT THE GROCERY STORE ...

In these uncertain times, your family can go a Year Without the Grocery Store!

While everything around us is in disarray and filled with confusion, you can take control of this area of your life and know that your family will have plenty of food, no matter what your circumstances. More importantly, if you're consistent, you can accomplish this **in fifteen minutes a day or less**!

Strapped for cash? Provide your family with a year's worth of food for $160 per person per year! I'll show you how.

In A Year Without the Grocery Store, I'll walk you through a **step by step** plan which:

- Incorporate the meals that your family already loves
- Takes into account your family's unique food **allergies, intolerances, and preferences**.
- Teaches you how to **economically store food** your family loves.
- Provides you with **simple recipes** using basic ingredients to make **comfort foods** that your family craves.
- Discusses alternate ways to cook your food storage in case you encounter an extended power outage.
- Instructs you how to **safely store** and **use stored water**.
- Points out **pitfalls and holes** in most people's food storage and **crafts a plan for how to avoid them.**

Don't know what you **don't know**? I help you **figure things out**! Discover the top **four food storage items most people miss**.

What often **overlooked item is essential for cooking** food storage?

What one type of item that most people forget can change the **same basic ingredients** into **totally different meals**? How does that work?

Never cooked without your stove? How do you **cook without a stove**? **I show you how**!

Be **better prepared** for other small emergencies with **bonus content** in this book including Kit Content Suggestions: BOB / 72 Hour Bag, car kit, power outage kit, sickness kit

Karen has been featured on Zero Hedge, The Organic Prepper, and Natural News. This authentic guide to food storage has been endorsed by Daisy Luther – The Organic Prepper.

Up your game and take care of your family **more comprehensively** so that your family can go A Year Without the Grocery Store. Pick up your copy on Amazon or other select retailers today!

STEP-BY-STEP INSTRUCTIONS TO TAILOR YOUR JOURNEY TO building your own stockpile of foods

Preparedness is kind of like blogging. It's a long journey with a steep learning curve! The whole purpose of this ***Companion Workbook to A Year Without the Grocery Store*** is to help level out that learning curve and create your own food storage plan.

This workbook...

- Walks you through setting up your long-term food storage.
- Takes you step by step through how to decide on your short-term food storage menu.
- Takes your menu and helps you break down each meal's ingredients.
- Gives you worksheets on which to collate the necessary foods for your short term-food storage.
- Provides eight checklists to give you suggestions for kits to help your family in crises large or small.
- Shows you how to determine your water needs and how to provide for those needs for your family.

This workbook is, as far as I know, the only product of its kind that **walks you step-by-step** through the process of **building your own stockpile of foods** that your family will eat and enjoy. The **worksheets** provide you with **point-by-point instructions** and give you **space to fill out your information**, to tailor this journey to meet your own particular needs. **Have a gluten issue? No problem!** You will choose your own shelf-stable foods that your family already eats. Really don't care for meat? No one's going to suggest that you eat it. Want to provide most of your own **fruits and veggies** from your **own garden**? Go right ahead. This workbook allows you to **customize this journey for YOUR family from start to finish**.

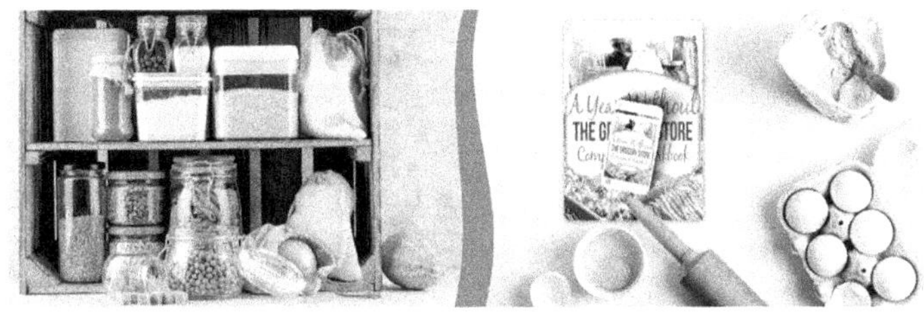

THE 2023 PREPPER PLANNER . . .

. . . is not just about filling your day with more things to do. It's about helping you to create focus on what is most important – for your family, for your work, for your preparedness, and for your ministry.

Do you ever feel that you wear so many hats (mom, wife, prepper, career, ministry) that you can't get everything that you need to get done – done. My crazy busy life requires a system to get things done. More importantly, I have learned not just how to get things done, but how to balance the different areas of my life at the same time.

What about you?

- Is life so full that you have a hard time getting necessary tasks done?
- Do you have multiple facets of your life that you need to balance?
- Do you have a hard time fitting purposeful preparedness into your schedule?
- Even if you have time for preparedness, do you struggle to know which preparedness activities should take priority?
- Do seasonal tasks – preparedness or otherwise – often fall by the wayside?

In the Prepper Planner You Get Everything You'd Expect from a Planner PLUS. . .

- An entire system to help you plan your day, week, month, season, and year!
- Monthly preparedness focus areas with suggestions on what To Learn, To Do, and To Buy.
- Step-by-step guidance on taking long-term goals and breaking them into bite-sized pieces.
- Advice on taking those bite-sized pieces and finding a way to fit them into your busy life.
- Monthly and Weekly priority pages and reflection pages
- Everything you need in ONE spot to make getting things done more streamlined.

Purchase your copy on LuLu.com or at AreYouPreparedMama.com today!

ENDNOTES

1.) Nathan Yao, “How Much More Time We Spent at Home,” FlowingData, accessed February 6, 2023, https://flowingdata.com/2021/09/03/everything-more-from-home/.
2.) Christie Bieber, “The Average Cost of a Wedding in 2020,” The Ascent, accessed February 6, 2023, https://www.fool.com/the-ascent/research/average-cost-wedding/
3.) “43% of U.S. homes are at high risk of natural disaster,“ Marketwatch, accessed February 6, 2023, https://www.marketwatch.com/story/43-of-us-homes-are-at-high-risk-of-natural-disaster-2015-09-03.
4.) Amazon, “Ohuhu Mini Camping Stove Solo Stoves,“ accessed February 6, 2023, https://amzn.to/3uJY5U6.
5.) Tiffany Means, ”Why Car Interiors Get so Hot in Summer,” Thought Co., accessed February 6th 2023, https://www.thoughtco.com/car-interiors-hot-in-summer-4056790.

BIBLIOGRAPHY

Amazon. "Ohuhu Mini Camping Stove Solo Stoves." accessed February 6, 2023. https://amzn.to/3uJY5U6.

Bieber, Christine. "The Average Cost of a Wedding in 2020." Last Revised September 2, 2020. https://www.fool.com/the-ascent/research/average-cost-wedding/.

Marketwatch. "43% of U.S. Homes Are At a High Risk of Natural Disaster." Last Revised September 3, 2015. https://www.marketwatch.com/story/43-of-us-homes-are-at-high-risk-of-natural-disaster-2015-09-03.

Means, Tiffany. "Why Car Interiors Get so Hot in the Summer." Last revised July 3, 2019. https://www.thoughtco.com/car-interiors-hot-in-summer-4056790.

Yao, Nathan. "How Much More Time We Spent at Home." Accessed February 6, 2023. https://flowingdata.com/2021/09/03/everything-more-from-home/.

www.ingramcontent.com/pod-product-compliance
Lightning Source LLC
LaVergne TN
LVHW010948110826
845149LV00015B/3257

* 9 7 9 8 9 8 8 5 4 3 8 1 7 *